THE ACCIDENTAL MAYOR

A Collection of Stories from the Side
Streets of Chinatown to the Main
Street of City Hall

DR. ED ENG

The Accidental Mayor: A Collection of Stories from the Side Streets of Chinatown to the Main Street of City Hall

Copyright @ 2022 by Edward Eng

All rights reserved in all media. No part of this book may be used or reproduced without written permission, except in the case of brief questions embodied in critical articles and reviews.

The moral rights of Edward Eng as the author of this work has been asserted by him in accordance with the Copyright, Designs, and Patents Act of 1988.

Published in the United States by BCG Publishing, 2022.

www.BCGPublishing.com

ISBN: 9781957255118

Notice: This book is a memoir. It reflects the author's present recollections of experiences over time. Some names and characteristics have been changed, some events have been compressed, and some dialogue has been recreated. Any views or opinions represented in this book are personal and belong solely to the author and do not represent those of people, institutions, or organizations that the author may or may not be associated with in a professional or personal capacity, unless explicitly stated. Any views or opinions are not intended to malign any religion, ethnic group, club, organization, company, or individual.

This book is dedicated to my parents, who made the sacrifice to come to this country in search of better opportunities for their seven children. They worked tirelessly in menial jobs to give us the privileged life that we now have. Thank you, Mom and Dad, for giving me the gift of grit that has helped me overcome countless obstacles. I am sad that my mom will not be able to read this book in person, but I know she will be looking down from heaven to share this achievement with me.

Thank you to my wife, Cathy, for your patience, encouragement, and confidence in me while I spent countless hours writing this book. You are an amazing partner. I am because you are!

Thank you to my son, Brandon, for your coaching and editing of this book. Your ambition, drive, and zest for life are the inspirational fuel for when I felt like giving up.

Thank you to my siblings for their unwavering support when I first ran for City Council. A special thank you to my sister, Vicky, who sacrificed her own career to become the main caretaker for both my parents so I could write this book without worrying about Mom and Dad.

Thank you to the residents of La Mirada. You have accepted me with open arms, and this sickly immigrant boy will be forever indebted to you.

Thank you to the mamacitas for showing up when others walked out. Your friendship will never be forgotten.

Thank you to my friend, Councilman Steve DeRuse, for choosing me, an unknown and someone you had never met before, as your commissioner when you had so many other viable choices.

TABLE OF CONTENTS

Foreword 1

PART ONE: THE IMMIGRANT JOURNEY

1. The Gold Mountain 14
2. Forever the Sickly Boy 26
3. Survival 33

PART TWO: BEYOND CHINATOWN

4. Becoming 81
5. The Coolidge House 86

PART THREE: THE THANKSGIVING MIRACLE

6. Catch of the Day 107
7. The Peruvian Rug 112
8. The Unbreakable Bond 117

PART FOUR: THE LOS ANGELES TIMES

9. The Metal Rice Bowl 134
10. The Executive 158
11. A Tale of Two Companies 166
12. The Expired Dream 170

PART FIVE: THE ACCIDENTAL MAYOR

13. My Training Ground 189
14. Serendipity 198

15. Not the Smiling Asian 205
16. The Capeless Heroes 216
17. A Historic Win 226
18. The Second Campaign 232
Reflection 245
About the Author 250

Accidental Mayor Philosophy: If you learn to leave room for unexpected surprises and stop trying to find clarity and justifications for all that is happening to you, life's biggest rejections will soon become your most spectacular stories. No single event on its own defines you, but together, all the pivotal moments become you.

FOREWORD

The *Accidental Mayor* is a book about grit and overcoming obstacles. It is my hope that the lessons in this memoir will inspire those who are struggling with life's curveballs and help people understand immigrant life differently. The goal of this book is not to pat myself on the back for delving into the world of politics, anyone with a passion for civic duty can do this. I want to use the stories of my journey to share a few tangible lessons I have learned and how these experiences have shaped my identity and philosophy on life.

My entire life and eclectic career path shaped my eventual journey into politics. If you had asked me years prior, I would have never believed it. These moments, as small as they were, have been defining moments of my life. I didn't write the script for how my life unfolded. In fact, the odds of me surviving the environment where I grew up and becoming a mayor of an American city were extremely low. A series of seemingly unrelated events that came together at the right time helped me accomplish something more significant than what I could have ever imagined. The fear of failure initially hindered my progress, but fortunately, life is not a one-shot deal. With every failure, I figured out how the world worked and was better prepared for each subsequent challenge. I learned from anyone willing to teach me, seized what opportunities I could muster, and never stopped pushing myself.

I finally understand that life is not a linear progression of steps, nor is it simple enough to explain in one event or phenomenon. We all want a straight path to success, but dreams and plans have an inexplicable habit of collapsing and manifesting themselves in unexpected ways. Everyone has a career they plan on achieving as a kid. Still, those aspirations never work out the way they were intended. There are disparaging events along the way that change the trajectory of your life. You don't know why they happened because you only realize how important they are much later, in some cases, decades later, and only then can you appreciate that it was a huge turning point. It is only in reflection that these disparate moments connect.

I would argue that no two lives are the same, and no life can be predestined, though science and computer programming have brought us closer to making reliable predictions. We all will experience some variations of "top-of-the-world moments" where we feel elated beyond imagination, such as getting married or seeing your child off to college. We will also experience "depths-of-the-earth moments" where we feel like our lives are nothing short of ending, such as getting fired from your dream job or having a family member pass away. In between these highs and lows, there exists inflection points that define the ascension to life's highs and the descension toward life's lows. We all will experience "in-between moments" in life, such as when you get a promotion, and then the next day your car breaks down (true story), or when one day you become a corporate executive, but the next day you don't have a job (also a true story). Life is the amalgamation of these experiences, and what defines our values are the unique meanings we assign to them.

If the value that holds true across lives is unpredictability, then the only reparation or solution we have is to alter the way we maneuver through life. Dire circumstances are never easy to endure. Nobody enjoys dealing with life's storms and setbacks. I am sure there are even moments everyone wishes they could forget and not have to relive. However, if you can persevere and grow through your circumstances, you are on your way to having a breakthrough. It all comes down to your perspective and what path you select after a failure. In life, nothing is ever wasted. Every seemingly trivial event or moment becomes a catalyst for something bigger. That is the accidental mindset. By tweaking our attitudes and developing our grit, we can ultimately create the best blueprint possible to help us navigate through unpredictability. Though I am only sixty-two, an age still viewed as relatively young in Chinese culture, my own life experiences have been marked by beautiful highs and plagued by the lowest of lows. These are the pivotal moments that defined who I am today and are a part of my journey to becoming The Accidental Mayor.

Using my own life as a case study, it is my sincere hope that this book will help free those who are shackled by the fear of failure to move forward and start embracing life's abundant opportunities. Stories and experiences like mine have not been heard enough throughout the history of America, and that's part of my responsibility. This is the collection of stories and lessons learned that defined who I am today and are a part of my journey from surviving the side streets of Chinatown to becoming a mayor of a city.

My starting point begins in Hong Kong.

PART ONE
THE IMMIGRANT JOURNEY

My humble upbringing has been my greatest strength. Witnessing the struggles of my parents was my becoming.

Mom

Dad

Dad and Ah Ngyin

What a Crybaby!

1st Grade

Our Family of 10

Leaving for the Gold Mountain

Golden Anniversary

1

THE GOLD MOUNTAIN

The Humble Beginning

The only barrier that kept me from quick death was a twelve-millimeter-thick acrylic shield. Pressing my face against the cabin windowpane, the buildings below looked like Lego building blocks. Within minutes, the plane had reached its cruising altitude of 36,000 feet. Overwhelmed with the sadness of leaving my paternal grandma, "Ah Ngyin", my vision began to blur, and I started sobbing uncontrollably. At nine years old, I had mixed emotions about leaving her; at the same time, I was excited about going to America, the country with the best schools, the most intelligent people, and the wealthiest businesses. To stop me from crying, my mom wiped my tears and snot away with her hand and whispered in my ear, "We are going to America, the land of opportunities. We will come back and visit soon." Those soothing words were like a shot of adrenaline through my body, and my distress was immediately replaced by exuberance. Slowly, my mind drifted to the last nine years of my childhood.

Everything for me began in Hong Kong. It was on this island that I developed a sense of identity. The culture of the Chinese population in Hong Kong was hallmarked by two distinct social features: the long work hours and the importance of familial ties. My family was no different. My parents immigrated to Hong Kong during the upheaval in China. They settled in Wan Chai District, now an upper-middle class neighborhood and a bustling part of Hong Kong. That wasn't how I remembered it, though.

We were at the lower rungs of the socio-economic spectrum of society, or as I called it, "barely enough money for food." At the time, my dad was a police officer who would be on his beat until the early hours of the morning, and my mom stayed home to care for all seven of us. Though I was young, I understood that my dad had to work long hours to keep a roof over our heads and enough food on the table. Because he was in law enforcement, we could live cheaply in a police dormitory apartment unit carved out of fifteen stories of concrete. Each level had thirty units that housed families ranging from five to ten in a household. It was not uncommon to have three to four generations living in the same home. I lived in Unit 88 with my parents, six siblings, my grandmother Ah Ngyin, and lizard friends wall-walking in plain sight.

Inside our dorm was 400 square feet of living space, equivalent to what we now call a studio pad. In the living room or multipurpose room as I would call it, my oldest brother and grandmother slept in their own army-type cot, which was so worn out that it sagged in the middle, almost touching the cement floor. The remaining five siblings divided a metal bunk bed which filled up most of the rest of the multipurpose room, with my two sisters sharing the bottom bed and three brothers fighting over the upper bed. I shared my parents' bed in a makeshift room constructed with three pieces of plywood with the wall as the anchor. In the corner was a stand-alone desk with four drawers that spilled over with clothes. My oldest brother's clothes occupied the top drawer, my sisters shared one, and the rest of the boys split the remaining. Occasionally cockroaches would find their way underneath all the valueless treasures inside each drawer; they made for fun surprises when we got dressed in the morning. The kitchen consisted of a small refrigerator, stove, and dining table that also functioned as a desk where we all did our homework. I would say we were minimalist, albeit not by choice. Even though we had only limited material comforts, it was the simple things in life that mattered most. No matter how busy we were, our family would eat dinner together every night without disruption. We did not have much, but it felt whole.

We always had a love-hate relationship with our neighbors. We didn't have a TV, so I would stand outside a neighbor's home before dinner and watch episodes of martial arts movies through their metal lattice screen door. These films all had the same storylines: the hero discovers the secret martial arts technique to avenge his family or loved ones and slashes his way into Chinese legend. When movies like *Crouching Tiger, Hidden Dragon* debuted in America, I was amused at how a pretty ordinary movie from my childhood took the country by storm. But none of the neighbors ever invited me inside their house to watch any of the episodes, even though we were considered friends. I would watch from outside until they slammed the door on me. I was probably invading their privacy, or more likely, because they were not able to charge for it. But it didn't bother me. We would fight with our neighbors one day, and then the next day, I was dispatched to borrow a spoon of sugar or salt from them. I suppose that is what families do.

On the eighth floor, the neighbors shared a common concrete hallway that stretched from one end to the opposite end, with families sharing communal bathrooms similar to that of college dormitories. The men's and women's restrooms were separated by ten square feet of metal chain-link fence that created overflow storage spaces assigned to each apartment unit. Families would use the extra amenity to hang their excess undergarments on bamboo sticks that doubled as weapons for kids and clotheslines for quick air-drying. Needless to say, we never felt alone or anonymous growing up in a co-housing environment.

Incongruous building exteriors were a hallmark of the Hong Kong architecture that I grew to love. The outside of our building had two separate personalities. Units that faced the street (ours included) had open space with unobstructed city views enclosed by four-foot cement walls. About 1,000 feet away, there were building facades adorned with vibrant signs, drawing chromatic inspiration from a Rubik's Cube, emblazoned with Cantonese characters. The uneven sawtooth skyline cut into the horizon in the background, which was far different from the neon flow of tourist hot spots and towering phalanxes of gleaming skyscrapers of the Wan Chai District you see today. Within one building alone, you could find at least three herbal healers (who doubled as doctors and shrinks) and a few seamstresses. If a portion of the building's real estate did not already have a vendor's neon sign, it instead was decorated with a spiderweb of scaffolding. There was always something to be fixed but rarely anyone doing the fixing. Neighbors would gather around to enjoy the sunset and watch the city lights in the evening. The only rule to remember was not to stick your head out because teenagers above would spit at those heads below. I followed these rules religiously, using the excuse that I was too short to see over the wall anyway, but in truth, it was because I was afraid of heights.

In contrast, the building's drab rear exterior wore a coat of creamy white paint that began to take on a sheen of yellow, most likely resulting from a poor Public Works Department and weather that ranged between beating sunshine and torrential rainfall. From a distance, the building appeared to have a freckled complexion: across its surface were dots of color, strewn in horizontal rows. Every day, you'd see each unit hang even more of their week's laundry across a network of clotheslines through a kitchenette space designed more for camp cooking. On my last visit in 2007, some of the buildings still displayed those cascading webs of clothes flapping in the wind.

As soon as you left the apartment building, you could feel the energy of the people hustling across streets with seemingly stalled construction sites at almost every intersection, and people carrying umbrellas to shield themselves from the perennial scorching heat or inclement storms. The streets were always crowded, and you could hear constant chatter along the way to your destination. With no lane dividers, traffic was extremely disorderly. Once the lights turned green, everyone pushed forward like a mob angling to cut one another off to get to their destination a few seconds faster. There was no personal space, and people moved ahead like a herd scrambling to cross the finish line.

Despite the unruliness of traffic and the seemingly millions of people occupying almost every square inch, amazingly, food vendors or Dai Pai Dongs found space in obscured alleyways. These Dai Pai Dongs were humble outdoor kitchens with nothing more than a gas-grill wok and a single wooden bench for sitting. Although not exceptionally nutritious nor known for their service and hygiene, these delicious cheap bites with simple culinary ingredients were the bedrock of heavenly outdoor casual dining of the Hong Kong food scene that I remembered. My favorite food memories were fried churro-like dough shaped like dog bones dipped in Jok (a bowl of plain rice porridge), and Won Ton Mein, noodles with delicious shrimp dumplings that simmered frantically over hot stoves. Together with a leaner version of the Dai Pai Dongs—just mobile carts with no benches that served only congealed pig blood shaped in squares, curry fish balls, or animal intestines on skewers, all mixed from the same soup base—these vendors characterized the gastronomic vibe of my old stomping ground. There were no Yelp recommendations or designated Michelin star chefs that drove foot traffic, and patrons just gravitated to their favorite Dai Pai Dong through word of mouth. On special occasions, we would celebrate at a Dai Pai Dong, and despite its low nutritional value, I always ordered my favorite dish of plain white rice showered with soy sauce and mixed with melted lard served on bamboo leaves. The ritual of churning the rice in the buttery lard and salty liquid until each grain got an even distribution brought me immense joy.

Recounting those endearing living conditions has helped me see the contentment found in simplicity. Despite our meager living conditions, I never felt that our lack of abundance was a significant issue because my neighbors all lived pretty much the same way minus a TV here and there. Other than the lizards that would scurry under the covers with me at night, the cockroaches that were rent-free guests in the clothing drawers, the light switch that did not activate the single light bulb hanging like a bat from the ceiling, or the glassless window in the kitchen that kindly invited nature in, I didn't feel malnourished or underprivileged. Simply put, we survived on what we had and did not yearn for what we did not.

We were unsophisticated and modest. But not only did I feel lucky, I felt safe. This feeling of security I attribute to my Ah Ngyin, who at the time was seventy-three years old. After over seven decades, she showed no physical effects of time. When most of my older neighbors walked with curved spines and supported themselves with a wooden crutch, Ah Ngyin had the posture of a lion, standing erect like the leader of a pack. While other seniors walked at a snail's pace up and down the stairs, she would beat me down eight flights of stairs. Whenever our neighbors yelled at the older kids for making too much noise in the hallways early in the morning, Ah Ngyin would chase down all of the nuisances and beat the respect out of them with her slippers and a shredded broomstick. She was more of an army general than a grandma, and I could not have loved her more.

As the youngest of my six siblings, Ah Ngyin took a keener interest in my well-being because I was diagnosed with a severe case of asthma at a very young age, and she probably felt that I would not be able to protect myself outside the tiny walls of our home. During fistfights with neighbors over noise and just the irritations of living in a crowded space, Ah Ngyin would bring out her wooden broom and start swinging like Jackie Chan. Except there was this one time when a teenager who knew martial arts took her broom away and pushed her back. Knowing that she was physically outmatched, she screamed, "You hit an old lady. I can't breathe." When all the neighbors heard the exaggerated commotion, they came out and shamed the juvenile into running away. I wanted to participate in the melee but didn't know how. She easily held me back with one hand, and at the same time, carried on a verbal assault even though her assailant was long gone.

Ah Ngyin and I developed a bond traditionally witnessed between mother and son. Every morning, she would help me get dressed in my limited collection of clothing, cook me breakfast, and walk me to school. No matter how far my school was, no matter the rain, and no matter the differences in our schedules, Ah Ngyin would be there every morning to take me to school and pick me up after school. Our walks became commonplace in my life, a comfortable routine that provided me with a sense of stability. Though her hands were weathered from years of labor, clasped in mine, they felt gentle and comforting. She made me feel more secure than any of my siblings did. Though physically she probably could not protect me, that paled in comparison to the emotional safety I felt in her presence.

During a routine afternoon, Ah Ngyin delivered the most heart-wrenching and life-changing news after picking me up from school. With happy tears rolling down her cheeks, she cried in Cantonese, "You're going to Gumshan (the Gold Mountain), you're going to America!" Not really understanding the gravity of the situation, I just jumped and screamed with her. She excitedly told me that Mom had received the news this morning that our visas were accepted and that we were headed to America, or as my friends and I had called it, the Gold Mountain. When I got home, I immediately ran to see my mom because I wanted to see what this powerful document looked like. Quickly, the initial excitement of moving to America subsided as I was internalizing that there were only nine visas, but our roof was home to ten. As I stood frozen trying to figure out the flawed math, Ah Ngyin enveloped me in her embrace, and with my face buried in her kind, warm stomach, she whispered, "Even though we are poor, your parents aspired for a better life for all of you. I hope we can rise out of our current economic situation by going to America. But I'm too old, and all of my friends are here. But I will miss you." With my ears cupped between her arms, her words sounded trapped underwater, drowning in a pool as I listened from the surface. I was distraught. I could not fathom leaving behind Ah Ngyin and living a soon-to-be luxurious life without her presence. My heart began shooting such a deep sadness all over my body and through my veins looking for a way out. The sign of sorrow manifested in a cascading waterfall of uncontrollable tears. Though my eyes were clenched shut, the tears burst at the seams and seared my cheeks. My head pounded. My ears burned fiery hot, and I felt like I could hear the color red.

In this fit of grief, I rushed to my room, looking for something to give Ah Ngyin as a memento of remembrance and a symbol of my love for her kindness. In Chinese culture, giving gifts is a ceremonial sign of respect. It was a mechanism that allowed Chinese people to demonstrate reverence for their elders and to show lasting commitments. Mixing tears and mucus from a slight cold, I presented Ah Ngyin with the plastic piggy bank that had housed my scholarship money to pay for my Jok splurges. In Hong Kong, free tuition was awarded to the top performer in each grade level, and luckily, my natural competitiveness and good study habits had kept me on top. It was symbolic of the love, appreciation, and respect for all the years she had taken care of me. We both knew it was not very much, but it was all I had. To make up for the paltry sum of money, I confidently told her, "I will pick up some gold coins and mail them back for you." A river of tears came down her face, and she said to me, "Thank you for your thoughtfulness. Study hard, go to a famous university, and get a good-paying job. I will look forward to hearing about your success."

That day was supposed to be the celebration of a new beginning, but for me, it meant that I would not see someone that I loved again for a long time. The sorrow I felt leaving her alone while I was promised a future of wealth was something that I could not grapple with. The sacrifices that she made for me when I had not yet demonstrated my worth to the world came from a place of pure love, and that moment taught me the importance of family.

It was in Hong Kong that I developed the strongest family ties. The emotional affliction of leaving Ah Ngyin became the first motivating force that drove me to do my best in any situation. I could not bear throwing away the opportunity to start life on top of the Gold Mountain knowing what my parents and Ah Ngyin had sacrificed for me.

In 1991, Ah Ngyin died at ninety-five years of age. To honor her, I promised myself that I would work as hard as humanly possible to make something of myself. For if I did not, the sacrifice and love my parents and Ah Ngyin spent on this sickly boy would be frittered away.

2

FOREVER THE SICKLY BOY

It was the first time I had been on a plane. I fought for the window seat because I wanted to see the world from high above. The pilot told us that we would arrive in America in approximately thirteen hours. It was a beautiful Thursday (February 27, 1969), a bit chilly, and I had on my brand-new sweater, ready for a fortuitous start in a new country.

Growing up, my understanding of America was informed by the stories that I had heard from my neighbors, who portrayed it as a beautiful place with lots of wealth. Ah Ngyin would describe America to me as the Gold Mountain, creating such a paradise out of a world and at the same time, raising expectations for things that were sensationalized. But an impressionable nine-year-old me actually believed that stepping off the plane, I would immediately be able to walk onto a gold-plated road that would eventually lead me to a shimmering mountain made of gold, and if I tugged at the precious metals hard enough, I could potentially end up with an endless supply of bullions. For me, America was idyllic. I believed that simply stepping foot onto the land would alter my life instantly. Silly? Yes, but America was the perfect utopia for us trying to claw our way out of poverty in Hong Kong.

Twenty minutes into the plane ride, the windowpane reflected my pathetic, sickly pale face. Sobbing quietly and trying not to be noticed, I saw my siblings talking and laughing in my peripheral vision. "He is crying again," my brothers sneered. But tears have their own mind independent of what the brain wants. While I was telling my tear ducts to stop, they refused to concede. Again, I proved to myself that I was sickly, weak, and flimsy. But as I looked out far away, I remembered imagining being rich and famous and by then, no one would know that I was weak and fragile. After all, I was going to the Gold Mountain, the land of dreams and hope. I would be all right.

But as the plane floated up and down, the thought of savoring the Gold Mountain did not help the nauseous feeling that was overwhelming me. Each bouncing motion triggered a queasy sensation in my stomach. I felt like I was in parallel universes. On the outside, my head felt an uncontrollable false sense of spinning motion. On the inside was the unsettling feeling of my stomach churning. I didn't really know how to deal with the onslaught of these symptoms since I had never been on an airplane before. It was much later that I found out this was called motion sickness.

To comfort me, my mom put White Flower Menthol liquid on my temples and then rubbed it gently on my throat to soothe me. The potion was supposed to be a magical Chinese cure-all remedy for every ailment on earth, but once again it did not work, and I started retching and vomiting uncontrollably all over my brand-new sweater. The kind stewardess brought me a bottle of water to calm my stomach and an air sickness bag as a cautionary measure, which minutes later, filled up with murky liquid, stinking up the airplane. I lurched forward and vomited some more as my mom calmly adjusted the bag to catch the foul-smelling fluid.

Embarrassed, confused, and sick, I felt helpless. My mom cleaned up my sweater and put more of this magic potion on me. The stewardess gave me a new vomit bag, told me to look out the window, and find a focal point far away to stare into. My mom then gave me a small vessel of Bo Jight Yuen, which is another panacea for all ailments. Together with the White Flower oil, it was a combination that was supposed to work for all aches and pains. But I continued to feel dizzy and nauseated.

The thirteen-hour plane ordeal added to my reputation as the sickliest member of the Eng family. I vaguely remember my brothers saying in disgust, "He cries over everything. He is so annoying!" I was always the weakest one of all my siblings. My mom used to say that she would rejoice and thank God if I went through one week without being sick. Growing up, I suffered from asthma, which would first turn into a cold, and then ultimately morph into a fever. It was a vicious cycle of germs, viruses, and bacteria attacking my immune system, which I had no defense against. I remember walking around with my arm in a sling for the longest time, but I don't remember how I injured it. It also didn't help my confidence that I was the shortest and lightest kid on our floor and possibly in the entire building. But I was always everyone's little brother, who by default, was included in every game.

The neighborhood kids I played with growing up were much older than me, but they were very nice to me and included me in every game, usually to help balance the team with the best athletes. We would all sit around in a circle while two team captains, usually the oldest kids, picked the teams. Once you got selected, you stood up and went over to your team. I would wait patiently to get chosen and always ended up the last one left sitting. I didn't care and I was game to participate as long as they were willing.

In relay races, I was always given a handicap of starting on the opposite end, only needing to run one leg of the race. When there was an odd number of people, the fastest guy would run an extra leg to balance my handicapped, shortened route. I was the excuse the losing teams used but I didn't care. I would talk up the game afterward and describe how we could have won and got everyone excited. In my scenario, it was never my fault but instead a trip here or a stumble there. Being picked last and losing are fine once you get used to it. It became normal after a while. I was just thankful that I was not excluded and was always an active participant.

I didn't like hide-and-seek because I was afraid of the dark. Between the women's and men's restrooms in our apartment building, it was usually very dark, with dim, flickering lights that made the hallway look like a scene from horror movies. I didn't want to be alone in the dark for an extended period during the game while others hid, and the game usually ended when the neighbors got bored of hiding without any action from me.

My favorite role was being an exuberant spectator in "cricket tournaments." It was more a grown-up pastime, but the diversion satisfied my emotional need to be socially accepted by the older kids. In addition, it was a good break from losing at the track relay or hide-and-seek. To get the show started, the handlers would bring in crickets in leaf-made habitats and transfer them into a big cardboard box disguised as a gladiator ring. There was no weigh-in to ensure that it was an equal fight like the UFC. During the prefight warm-up, the contestants would tickle their competing crickets' antennas with straw feathers until they became aggressive. When both crickets were sufficiently agitated, the divider was lifted, and they would start fighting until a winner was declared. Winners were given nicknames and losers sent the competitors on a pilgrimage to find the next cricket with big potential. I would sit on the shoulders of my brother or one of the older kids, where I would scream and howl throughout the combat. I would cheer the loudest, walk like a peacock, and talk smack when my brother won. I guess it was about family pride.

For my seventh birthday, my older brother brought me a pretty good-sized, thick-necked cricket with the intent of encouraging me to move from being a spectator to a participant. However, I ended up treating the insect like it was my pet rather than a potential champion. I kept it in a plastic jar and let it crawl on my hands and tickle me with its pointy spikes. To me, they were beautiful, harmless, and gentle, and I didn't want to let it fight and potentially get hurt. But the incessant chirping got pretty annoying, especially at night, and I was asked to involuntarily jettison my first pet. While I continued to partake in neighborhood games as a spectator, I was growing tired of being viewed as the "sick and weak" kid.

After the brutal fourteen-hour plane ride, we landed at LAX. My mom's brother, Uncle Frank, who was already in the US and had been working for years to secure visas for our family, was there to pick us up in his blue station wagon. Two of my older cousins were also there to greet us. I clandestinely checked them out and measured myself against them physically, and to my disappointment, they were much bigger and taller than me. I don't think there was a seat belt law at the time because we ended up fitting thirteen people in his vehicle with six kids in the very back. That was the first time I had ever ridden a car.

I looked out the window and the blue sky was postcard-perfect, but pockets of dark clouds were quickly forming. It began to drizzle and as the rain became more intense, the heavy drops were drumming against the car like a rock band. I was mesmerized by the windshield blades working synchronously to remove the rain strumming against the glass like a musical chime. But only ten minutes into my first car ride, I started to feel queasy. Once again, the spinning motion in my head working in unison with my retching stomach created a nauseating sensation. I told my mom I was not feeling well, and she told my uncle to pull over. I hurtled out of the car and puked on the side of the road. My eyes began welling up from embarrassment, I clenched my jaw and blinked as fast as I could to keep the salty water from seeping out. But it just didn't help. Unfortunately, the rain was not enough to hide the tears. My uncle gently asked me, "Why are you crying?" Immediately my mom responded, "He is not crying. The wind blew dust into his eyes, and he was blinking to try to get the particles out." My mom was trying to pass it off as reflex tears caused by irritating dust specks that didn't exist. I was a wimp. Not only was I already known as the weakest in the family and the entire dormitory in Hong Kong, in just a short ten-minute car ride, I had cemented my legacy as the weakling among all the cousins too.

3

SURVIVAL

The Gift of Grit

Upon setting foot in America in 1969, I had hoped to be greeted by a glistening mountain with unprecedented amounts of gold. Instead, what I had dreamed to be the Gold Mountain turned out to be a dull, flat tarmac called LAX. My new home was Chinatown, Los Angeles, a thirty-minute walk from downtown. It was an old community with a traditional identity predominantly occupied by Chinese immigrants. Established herbal shops and markets, primarily owned by earlier Chinese settlers, helped new immigrants feel a sense of belonging and familiarity. Chinatown also mirrored Hong Kong, having buildings with plastered neon signs declaring Chinese culture along every street, and at every corner, there were clotheslines drooping across the sides of apartment buildings, with over-exaggerated frowning faces giving personality to the lifeless structures.

On its surface, Chinatown attempted to emulate its source material in every way possible. Conceptually, the move from Hong Kong to Chinatown should have been a seamless cultural transition. In both cities, I was surrounded by people who looked like me, spoke like me, and probably shared similar familial values. But despite these congruences, Chinatown felt so indescribably foreign, more like a bootleg designer shirt with the brand's name spelled wrong. The perception that when an immigrant comes to America, life is miraculously or instantaneously better is truly misunderstood. It was not that we dismissed cultural ties with one another; rather, I believe it was a shared conscious fear of living without understanding the opportunities or ecosystems of our new environment. Our worldview was basically limited to what we saw in the mirror.

When we first arrived, we only spoke Cantonese and Hoi San, my parents' native dialect from an old village in China. Their English deficiency meant many corporate opportunities were closed to them in the US. My dad went from solving crimes and locking up bad guys in Hong Kong to working as a dishwasher and custodian to support his burgeoning family. He had multiple slipped discs and a spinal fusion from his days as a cop and bending over for extended periods cleaning toilets and scrubbing dishes aggravated his old injuries. My mom was a self-taught seamstress at a sweatshop hidden in a dead-end street underneath an overhead ramp. I remember she was getting paid around twenty-five cents for sewing seams and could earn an extra thirteen cents for putting on a zipper. My eldest brother and my oldest sister also had to work to supplement the family income, cover the most basic necessities, and make ends meet. I will forever remember their selfless acts and sacrifices so that I could have a better opportunity at life than they did. By any economic measure, we lived below the federal poverty level and were identified in the lower rungs of the social spectrum. I vividly remember that in the rare times we could go out to eat at a restaurant in America, we always drank water and always skipped dessert. Because of our language barrier, we didn't know what our rights were or how to access social services from the government. But even if the services were readily available, our family's pride would have kept them away from seeking assistance. In Chinese culture, asking for help diminishes your value, and they didn't want to be judged or humiliated.

Despite the financial hardship, gruesome work schedule, and discomfort my parents had to endure, I never saw anything but hope in their eyes, even though I am sure they carried the weight of uncertainty and fear about the future. Their adverse circumstances tested their physical, mental, emotional, and spiritual strengths, but I never saw them indulge in self-pity. My parents didn't have big dreams for themselves because they were constantly in survival mode. My dad once told me, "When you are a foreigner in a new country, you are the ultimate outsider trying to assimilate and adapt. Big dreams are just a luxury for the rich. For the rest of us, you just continue grinding to overcome repetitive obstacles that push you beyond your comfort zone, and then you begin accepting discomfort as part of life." I believed in those words, but more importantly, I believed in the actions associated with those words. If you strip away all the theoretical constructs on grit from academic research, what I saw was a daily exhibition of courage and resilience, a manifestation of a level of pain tolerance above what the average person can withstand, and an embodiment of the human capacity to adapt during dire circumstances.

Although I did not get the kind of career guidance that kids receive today because my parents did not finish elementary school, they demonstrated the most enduring leadership lesson I could not have learned from books: unwavering determination in the face of adversity, also known as grit. My parents had overcome insurmountable odds to raise seven children in a foreign country with a crippling language barrier, and they kept moving forward with a singular and unchanging purpose: providing something better for their children. They proved that it is possible to start with nothing, overcome obstacles, and achieve a dream of giving their children the opportunity to live a life better than they had. Instead of running away from the unfamiliar and unknown, they fought through everything life put in front of them.

Their gift of grit was the most treasured present I have ever received from them. It was better than inheriting millions of dollars. I just didn't expect I would have to unwrap my present and apply it as fast as I had to before I grew into adulthood.

"See You After School"

As thankful as I was to be in America, life was immediately difficult. Despite not having much in Hong Kong, I found success in academia and solace in my grandmother. In America, I did not understand the former, and I was completely without the latter.

My first childhood house was 808 Barlett Street, an older but decent-sized house situated between two abandoned lots with overgrown weeds sprawling out like a cornfield. We would play hide-and-seek behind the thicket of brushes, but I would erupt in hives after each game. I just couldn't understand why I was the only one who reacted with rashes or why my eyes swelled up from the pollen. But rather than taking allergy medications, I simply waited it out. I took comfort in the fact that my mom always told me that I would eventually outgrow my compromised immune system.

Unfortunately, my health never improved much, and I was still always sick. With no health insurance, we went to the neighborhood Chinese doctor located in downtown LA, who would always give me a shot (not sure what it was, but he said it would make me stronger), and then prescribed Dimetapp to relieve my chronic asthmatic condition. Perhaps breathing in the bountiful fresh air in America and consuming more nutritious food, I would be stronger in no time, and no one in my new school would even know that I was a sickly boy.

Nevertheless, I was very optimistic and excited. My vision and expectation of what America was supposed to be—running hot water, private bathrooms, and prompt trash pickup—all came true. I started tracking my height against the kitchen wall, and every time it went up by a minuscule 1/32 of an inch, I was ecstatic, believing that I was on my way to a growth spurt. I just couldn't wait to rid my identity of being weak and frail. I was ready for a healthier version of myself in a new school.

I tossed and turned all night, excited to go to an American school, learn English, and make new friends. I shared a bed with my older brother and woefully for him, my commotion kept him up through the night. He finally threatened to beat me up if I did not stay still. I think he was also perturbed because he had to sleep next to his perpetually sick brother with a mild fever. I slept in a mummy position for the rest of the night, hoping I would not get smacked. I woke up with a stiff neck but was excited for a new beginning since no one in my school would know that I was unhealthy. I hummed a medley of Beatles songs while the birds outside tweeted in harmony as I welcomed the promise of a new day.

My introduction to an American education came at the gates of Castelar Elementary School in the heart of Chinatown. Thinking back, the architecture of Castelar resembled that of any ordinary rectangular building but with an added Asian flair on its exterior, sort of like a Panda Express. The front of the school was marked with a piercing red wooden edifice that rose almost two stories high, transforming a blank exterior into a pagoda entrance. To the left of the wooden pagoda, an equally red iron gate led into the belly of the school. Oddly, the entrance to Castelar felt so much more Chinese than the primary school I attended back in Hong Kong, which was quite plain.

I started school in the third grade. The school was filled with predominantly Chinese immigrants and a few Hispanics sprinkled in here and there. Immediately, I noticed that I was the shortest and skinniest boy in class. I thought that my physique must have been because of my diet in Hong Kong, and I would eventually catch up physically to the rest of my classmates. I also noticed that the hierarchy of authority in the school system was drastically different. In Hong Kong, teachers had full control and command of their classrooms, and they were free to smack me with a ruler or yank my hair if I talked during class. But in America, kids would talk and make noises throughout the day while in the classroom without any consequences. In America, parents and adults had all the power. But because my parents were so unavailable due to work and being limited with the English language, they had no voices in school.

Another contrast was that in Hong Kong, we stayed in one classroom and different teachers rotated in and out for separate subjects. In America, we had a homeroom and then went to various classrooms for other subjects. The stark difference had dire consequences—it made the hallways dangerous. The big man on campus would walk right in the middle of the hall, and I would walk on the side near the lockers, otherwise I got knocked over. In Hong Kong, the most popular kids were scholars, but in America, the most popular kids were athletes, which didn't bode well for me.

While I did not speak too much English, for the most part, I could understand the majority of what was being taught. Tasks in the classroom were pretty straightforward: adding transition words between paragraphs, using proper punctuation to express my ideas, and learning an array of writing styles. However, what turned out to be the most arduous task, at least for me, was my pronunciation and speaking. While I could read and write sufficiently, the bane of my primary school existence was my inability to "properly" deliver discernable sentences. The language barrier led my teacher to believe that I was not competent in the material she taught. You would think that in a school attended by a community full of immigrant children in Chinatown, teachers would be a bit more understanding of my inability to speak English.

Math class proved to be an ally. American third-grade math was still focused on basic skills and understanding of numbers: knowing the names of decimal places, adding four-digit numbers, calculating perimeter and area, multiplying multi-digit numbers, and mental addition and subtraction. While this material was probably new for many students, what I learned up until second-grade math in Hong Kong was years ahead of what was being taught in the Castelar classroom. For me, numbers were my first language. While I struggled with complex sentences, I could multiply over eight-digit numbers. When I commonly forgot silent letters, I never failed to "carry the one" when dividing. Though I had difficulty reading a long sentence aloud, I could easily calculate a number well into the thousandth place.

The language barrier kept me from making new friends, and desperate to accelerate my command of English, I would intentionally pay attention to the mouth movements of the kids in the class and try to silently mimic the sounds I heard. A mouthy kid named Carlo took issue with my "mimic method." During a routine morning recess, I went to the bathroom, and the next thing I knew, the bathroom door slammed shut behind me. As I turned back to see who had closed the door, there was Carlo staring at me. I smiled at him and waved hello, and without any warning, he charged toward me, bear-hugged me, picked me up off the ground, and slammed me to the concrete floor. While lying on the cold cement in distress, he gave me an extra kick for good measure before he left. It is worth noting that Carlo was about five inches taller than me and outweighed me by about thirty pounds. I went back to the classroom, and no one asked why my t-shirt was dirty or why I was limping. He stood over me and told me never to stare and mock him in the classroom again. In reality, I was just trying to understand what he was saying since I didn't speak any English at the time. I was naïve to believe that school would be a secure space to safely grow into adulthood; instead, it was a dangerous environment, especially for immigrants.

A month later, I angered the school's big shot, Peta, who stood five-feet-three-inches tall and was stronger than anyone else in the school. He also had a menacing mustache and was popular with all the girls. It was rumored that his actual age was five years older than what he had claimed. He didn't like the fact that our classroom had beaten his classroom in punchball, and I must have shown too much exuberance because he accused me of taunting him. He shoved me, grabbed my sweatshirt, and pinned me against the fence. Luckily, the bell rang and saved me. "See you after school!" he snarled. Those were the four words I dreaded most throughout elementary school. I was so scared the rest of the day and took a different exit out of the school to avoid him. I remembered praying to God to help me grow taller and get stronger fast.

A couple of days later, he tracked me down, pushed me, and tried to goad me into a fight. I knew I was no match for him, so I just kept walking while everyone was taunting me and calling me a chicken. He tormented me for about a week and sensing that I was too scared to fight him, he finally stopped. One afternoon, I followed him home from a distance and made sure I knew where he lived. I made a promise that I would challenge him to a fight in front of his house when I got taller, but my promise never materialized since we became friends in junior high school (he never grew another inch, but I did).

As I became more mature, I realized that holding on to these negative thoughts was unproductive and harmful for my emotional health. It was important to forget what hurt me, but it was even more important never to forget what those moments taught me. My best revenge was to become as successful as possible and not worry about things that didn't really matter.

I wasn't the only one getting bullied. On a routine day walking home with my brother, waiting around the corner about 100 feet from our house were these two guys, Miguel and Santiago. Without any forewarning, Miguel tackled my brother, took him to the ground, and mounted him. The fight did not end there though, Miguel started to lift my brother's head up and repeatedly banged the back of his head onto the cement. All this time, I was restrained by his taller and bigger friend, Santiago. Hoping to get the attention of some good Samaritan in the normally busy street, I started screaming at the top of my lungs in my high-pitched prepubescent voice. The piercing sound must have startled Santiago, because he loosened his grip for a second, long enough for me to wiggle away and run toward my brother. Miguel got off my brother and said something unintelligible to us. I knew we were outmatched and did not talk back to him. I helped my brother up, picked his books up off the ground, and walked home together. Occasionally, I would look back to make sure they didn't follow us.

That night, I was upset that I was not able to jump into the fracas and help my brother fight these thugs. We never talked about why they were waiting to pick a fight with us. I can only imagine what my other siblings were going through in middle and high school, where the boys were bigger, stronger, and more hostile. I remember that was the day I started to consistently track my growth several times a day against the kitchen wall.

It was not a promising start for us. Despite high grades on math exams, I was held back from advancing to the fourth grade because of my weakness in English. To say I felt disappointed was an understatement. To come to a new country anticipating a better life and instead be told you are too dumb to move forward with your education because of a misperception of your ability to converse was the exact opposite of what I had envisioned my life in America to be. I felt like a failure, not just to myself but to my parents. Education was our way to become upwardly mobile. That summer, between third and fourth grade, I studied English voraciously, and based on my marks on reading and writing tests, I knew I understood the material, but I had to figure out how to demonstrate it to my teachers.

During my second try at third grade, Ms. Cohen, my new teacher, met with the administrative staff and argued that my math skills far exceeded all the third graders in the class. Because of my age, she recommended that I skip fourth and go directly into the fifth grade. From that point onward, I knew that I had to give more than 100 percent of myself in anything I did. I felt that if I did not give my maximum effort, my parents' sacrifices would be futile. Getting held back in the third grade ingrained within me the importance of education. I have no doubt in my mind that these occurrences did not happen by mistake. Although these moments at the time were world-shattering, without them, I don't think I would have developed the motivation to push forward in life.

I first became friends with Wai in fifth grade. He was easily the most intelligent kid in the class, and I was hoping that a sliver of his intelligence would trickle down to me by osmosis. We became best friends and spent almost every hour of the day together. Together, we walked to school, ate lunch, walked home, and then hung around at his house for a couple of hours to talk about our crushes before I proceeded home. I would then walk alone up the hilly concrete jungle, jump a few fences, hop on block walls, and pick a few apples, oranges, and apricots off people's trees before arriving home. I called it the "nourishment path."

My friendship with Wai was amazing. I credit him for refining my brain and giving it an upgrade. He was easily the top student in every subject in class, a great artist, and a real-life MacGyver. This guy solved problems in 3-D while the rest of us were still trying to figure out what 2-D looked like. On days when I played basketball until late at night, I would copy his homework while he painted my art projects for me. He was already six foot two by the time we were in sixth grade and was a good-looking young man. I was about five foot two and, according to my mom, fairly good-looking too.

One afternoon, on our way home from school, a pickup truck screeched right next to us and stopped. The uncle of one of our classmates got out of the truck, grabbed Wai's backpack, and shook everything loose until all the schoolbooks fell on the burning concrete. He proceeded to grab Wai's jacket collar and threw him to the ground. With a crowd surrounding us at this point, he proudly stood over Wai as if he was a gladiator and threatened him to never tease his niece again (apparently Wai made a joke about our classmate, Susan, and she told her uncle). He continued the verbal assault until he ran out of breath.

Angry that a grown man would pick on kids, I lunged toward him and threw a punch toward his face, but my T-Rex arms missed the target by at least a foot. He looked at me, laughed, and ignored me. I was really insulted that I seemed invisible to this thug. I would rather have been beaten up than be invisible. He turned to me and made a sudden motion as if he was going to hit me, and instinctively, I flinched and ducked at the air punch but immediately regretted my action. Then he laughed and said, "Look for me when you grow another foot, kid. I will be waiting for you." I turned to help Wai up, and we both cried on the way home. Wai said he wanted to be alone, so I went home via my traditional route, jumping fences and climbing on block walls to grab a few fruits here and there. We broke our routine that day.

The weight of embarrassment and anger affected me the rest of the day. I was angry that we were bullied, but I was more furious that no one intervened to help two twelve-year-old boys getting harassed by a grown adult. After all the rage subsided, I felt scared and helpless. My small stature and limited arsenal of physical attacks did not give me many options to deal with aggressors. I told myself that I would one day avenge the unprovoked assault for my friend.

We continued to walk home on the same streets after school, and the punk harassed us for a couple more days with stare-downs and indignant laughter as he followed us in his pickup truck. After seeing that we were pretty powerless, he moved on after a few more days of taunting. But being defenseless twelve-year-old kids, you just learn to let go, aspire to be better and not bitter. My revenge evolved from beating up the hoodlum to dreaming about where we would be twenty years from now. I was sure Wai would be some genius inventor headlined on the cover of *Forbes*, and I would be somebody other than a truck driver looking for kids to beat up.

The following week, Wai built a lateral pull-down machine with old bicycle parts using chains and spoils as the piston mechanism. We added muscle building to our daily routine, and while he got muscular quickly, I gave up after a few uses. Bodybuilding was just not something I enjoyed. Wai definitely shaped my worldview and upgraded my intelligence level from limbic to neocortex level. I will forever miss those childhood moments growing up and hanging out with him.

After forty years, we finally reconnected through Facebook, and although he was never featured in *Forbes*, he more than lived up to my expectations of him. He was insanely successful as an inventor, entrepreneur, and corporate executive, and I think I did okay too.

Alpine Playground

Eventually, basketball became my refuge. In Hong Kong, recess consisted of jumping jacks, rope climbing, and running. In America, you choose one of four games to play at recess and lunch: tetherball, four square, punchball, and basketball. I chose basketball to be my sport because it allowed physical contact. I quickly discovered that I was a decent athlete with speed and agility. I got good at ball handling and had a knack for creating my own shots from any angle. I played against older kids and more than held my own. I would play basketball after school from 3 p.m. to 6 p.m. every night. On weekends, the neighborhood kids and I would look for portable basketball hoops or rims mounted on top of garages where we could play. Most families were kind enough to let us play for an hour or two, but when we monopolized their garages all afternoon, they would politely ask us to leave. We would then look for another house to play at.

As my confidence grew from basketball, my physical health also improved. I enjoyed the game so much that I would play through fevers, and for the first time in my life, I was always picked first. However, my newfound basketball skills also attracted unwelcome trouble from school bullies. During a routine recess in school, I embarrassed Daniel, a tall fifth grader and one of the leading bullies of the school, by outscoring him. I played through the intentional fouls and swipes aimed at my face instead of the basketball and still scored at will in front of the school crowd. After the game, he just tackled me, mounted me, slapped me around, and spit on me in front of a growing crowd of spectators. Fortunately, I was saved by the bell. Daniel and his cronies would bump me, yank my hair, and take my lunch for a couple of weeks. A month later, I saw him mounted in the same position that he had me in by a much larger student outside of school. He was unable to move with each arm trapped underneath the knees of this guy, and with punches raining down on him, he said, "No more!" He was a bloody mess, and both eyes were swollen shut. I never saw him again for the rest of the school year. Every day was about surviving the law of the jungle, ruled by strongest, meanest, and baddest bully.

At this point, I was beating everyone in one-on-one basketball at school, and I wanted to play against better competition. Alpine Playground, the only neighborhood park in Chinatown, was located directly across the street from Castelar Elementary School. Alpine was where all the older kids hung out after school. There were eight outdoor basketball hoops on cracked cement and an indoor gym. The playground was always crowded. The perimeter of the park was lined with cars twenty-four hours a day. The park had familiar features: streetlights, a few metal benches, swings, old men playing chess, and sneakers squeaking loudly from the indoor gym.

There were no referees, so very few fouls were called. There were no participation trophies. If you won, you played again. If you lost, you were forced to watch for hours before you could play again. Sometimes the person who called the next game would pick good players from the losing team, and the same guys got to play all the time. Each Saturday and Sunday morning, the games started at 9 a.m. and lasted until the gym closed at 9 p.m. You had to be good in these types of pick-up games to be playing all day. The not-so-good players or younger kids would play at the outdoor courts, and the older and better players got to play indoors. That was the hierarchical playground structure and unspoken rule.

Even though the playground was infested with gangs and fights would break out throughout the day, I would play two to three hours every day, rain or shine. I didn't know it at the time, but it was a passion with a capital P! The day was too short, school too long, and time went by too fast. I finally drummed up enough courage to go inside the gym and watch the middle and high school kids play.

Early one Saturday morning, I was given a chance to play when only nine players showed up at the gym. I more than held my own and started playing there regularly. I excelled and became one of the best younger players in the playground. I would play against kids three to four years older and stood my ground. I was still physically small, but basketball made me feel strong and valued. But I will never forget what it felt like to get picked last and would always choose the less skilled kids, knowing that I would be able to balance the teams with my abilities. Feeling more self-assured than ever, I was prepared to test my skills against older and bigger boys in junior high school. For the first time in my life, I felt confident in something. I stopped getting sick. Maybe it was just my body maturing, but I think the mental aspect had just as much to do with it. Passion also attracts people and opportunities. My growing skills began attracting coaches and mentors.

"Where You From?"

In the '70s, mandatory busing programs were passed as a way to ensure racial equality and integration in California. Students in the Los Angeles Unified School District were assigned to either a school within or outside their neighborhoods to diversify the racial makeup of classrooms as part of the compulsory busing mandate. Some of my friends were bused to schools in the Valley, which was way outside of our neighborhood, and for the rest of us Chinatown kids, it was only 2.5 miles to Nightingale Junior High School. The school was named after a British nurse who demanded the best sanitary conditions and practices for her patients. But her legacy did not reflect the school's conditions then. At the time, Nightingale was predominantly Hispanic, and the influx of Chinese immigrants fueled gang wars not only between Hispanics and Asians, but even within the same racial communities.

It was survival of the fittest. Gangs ruled on campus. They wanted you to be afraid of them. The tension would quickly escalate with an unintentional stare in the wrong direction, a walk of perceived overconfidence, an inadvertent gesture, or irrepressible laughter. The school was more like a sanctioned UFC fight with the perimeter fence serving as the octagon cage, except there was no floor padding, no rules, no referees, and always a cheering audience. The campus was a battle royale spiraling out of control. Scuffles broke out daily on the bus to and from school, in the playground, in lunch areas, and on occasions, inside the classrooms. Some fights continued onto the streets after school. I had my fair share of fights but unfortunately, I ended up mostly losing. I was not a natural-born fighter. I learned how to fight by imitating techniques from Bruce Lee movies which did not work for me in actual hand-to-hand combat.

I remember being beaten up in drafting class by a ninth grader because I refused to respond to him when he asked me, "Where you from?" He was over six feet tall and punched me about six to seven times before I even had a chance to defend myself. He grabbed me, threw me on the ground, held me down, and kept punching me until I was practically unconscious. He kept yelling at me, "Where you from?!" I refused to concede and bit my lip until it was a bloody mess. I was not going to give in to this bully. My teacher, Mr. Merlo, saw what was happening and ran over to pull him off of me. He proceeded to ask this guy to apologize to me, and the hoodlum just laughed and walked out of the classroom. In the bathroom, the mirror reflected a battered face and bloodied nose. Tears were streaming down my cheeks, but I felt strong. I was aching in places that I didn't know existed, yet my self-esteem was intact. I stood up to a bully, and I was still standing, although the debilitating pain felt otherwise.

To avoid more pain of getting mauled in the confined spaces in the back of buses, which limited our ability to run, my friends and I decided to walk to school instead. The decision to walk meant we had to get up earlier to make up time for the bus ride. But being young, we loved to explore even though sometimes it was potentially dangerous. One morning, we found a large hole in a chain-link fence that was meant to shield pedestrians from venturing into the river. Of course, we went through the hole and found a parallel path along the Los Angeles River, which eliminated waiting at traffic lights and cut down our foot commute by twenty minutes. But more importantly, we didn't have to cross all the avenues.

The biggest school fight occurred when older gang members came onto the campus and started a massive brawl against an opposing gang. All the exits were choked off by pupils scrambling to get out. Students were crying, running downstairs, and colliding with those who were scuttling upstairs. We looked like ants being interrupted and scurrying in all directions to get out. It was chaos all over the school. Because I panicked and was running, gangs started chasing me, and as I looked around, the only clear path was toward the women's gym. I saw the women's PE teacher, and she waved at me to run toward her. She told me to run inside, locked her office door, and like a real-life guardian angel, stood by the door with an aluminum baseball bat, ready to stop anyone from coming in. I escaped unscathed in the biggest riot of the year. Some of my friends were not so lucky, and they ended up with busted noses and broken ribs.

The violence and racial tension were not just confined to the inside boundaries of the school. Outside of the school campus, mayhem erupted during some of the most prominent ethnic celebrations, such as Nisei Week and Chinese New Year. But we still celebrated our culture despite the lurking danger. During one of the Nisei Week celebrations, a man was beaten to a pulp just for laughing too loud. A group of gangsters confronted him, rained punches on him, and then threw a metal trash can on him to cap off the beating. With his face battered and blood pouring from his nose and mouth, he was just lying there motionless. The cops came and asked if anyone saw anything. Although I recognized one of the kids from my school, I was too scared to say anything.

To avoid physical beatings and verbal harassment, we would stick together like a pack of wolves to give the impression that we were a pseudo gang capable of protecting ourselves from danger. We first dropped off the friends who lived closest on our route home, and as usual, I would hang out with my best friend Wai at his apartment, where we would talk about our dreams of just getting out of this neighborhood. We didn't really fantasize about anything else. Before dark, I would use side streets and little-known alleyways to reduce my exposure to gangs since I was going home alone.

During the calmer moments (which were few and far between), other teens would mock us by pulling back the corners of their eyes using their index fingers until the shape of their eyes looked like a single line. That was their interpretation of what Asians looked like. They would follow it up with unintelligible sounds imitating our language. My brothers suffered similar fates. I saw firsthand one brother getting beaten up in a theater and another extorted for money from his hard-earned job.

School was supposed to be a safe haven, not a battlefield, but the system didn't shield us from the brutality of the gang wars. The *"See you after school"* phrase from elementary school was now replaced by the more violent *"Where you from?"* as the most dreaded slogan. Although *"Where you from?"* needed a linking verb to make it grammatically correct, the catchphrase represented pervasive words whose delivery immediately caused a sense of heightened anxiety. One wrong response to this axiom could escalate into a violent brawl.

That was the immigrant experience growing up in the '70s. We were just prisoners of the new environment, trying to adapt to the immigrant life. We had to grow up quickly, but we survived!

The Scar

One of the worst days I can remember was when my friends and I skipped school to go to the beach. It was a sunny afternoon. The eight of us jammed ourselves into Wai's little brown Pinto and headed down to the beach for some four-on-four football. Just ten minutes into the game, we saw a bunch of teenagers headed our way. I must have stared at them for a second too long because they headed straight toward me. Before I could defend myself, I felt excruciating pain in the temple area above my right eyebrow, and then I fell onto the ground. The taste of sand, rocks, and seashells isn't so pleasant when it fills your mouth. I blacked out momentarily, then I felt blood pouring down my face like a faucet, and the next thing I knew, I was in Wai's car, headed to the nearest hospital. The pain was all-consuming, from throbbing in my head all the way to a searing, blinding agony. However, the doctors could not do anything because we were all underage. When my parents finally arrived, I lied and told them I had gotten hurt in our football game. In reality, it was from the hook of a belt knuckle.

Lying down on the operating table and staring at the surgical light above me, the doctor began sewing stitches on my right eyebrow to seal the cut, and sensing that I was wincing in pain, he asked if I needed more anesthetics. I declined because I didn't want to be a weakling anymore. Instead, I started singing "Reasons" by Earth, Wind & Fire to take the focus off the sting. But the pinches from the last three threads pulling the edges of the cut together shot up my face like fire and made me dizzy. When the final surgical knot was tied on my wound, I felt like someone took a part of me and then put it back the wrong way.

The dried blood was gone, and the pain had faded to a dull throb. The tears had disappeared. I fiddled with the stitches, being careful not to irritate the wound. The cut left a scar above my right eyebrow. With no medical insurance to cover the surgery, I understood that my family was not in a position to afford the procedure and probably had to use up all their emergency savings. I felt terrible that my parents had to spend their hard-earned money on an unworthy kid like me. I imagined that if I was in Hong Kong, at least the expenses for the operation would be covered. But they never complained once. Their love for me really shined through in that moment. I felt so helpless and frustrated but didn't know what to do to relieve the burden they were carrying. I knew I had to make a drastic change in my life.

My ignorance in skipping school and putting myself in unnecessary danger resulted in an added burden to the already paltry income needed to feed a family of nine. Not only was I not contributing any value to the family, but I was now adding to their financial distress. I was ashamed of myself but vowed someday to acquire the skills necessary to defend myself (today I have a purple belt in Brazilian Jiu-Jitsu [BJJ] and have trained and sparred with professional Muay Thai, kickboxing, and Taekwondo fighters). With tears welling up, I also solemnly promised that my kids would never have to grow up in this kind of turbulent environment and I would have a voice in this world.

I was emotionally exhausted. We lived in a combustible environment, and violence continued to plague the community throughout my middle school years. Bullies could sniff out fear and insecurity from an avenue away. It was far from the yellow privilege that the media had portrayed of successful Asian Americans. Even during the crescendo of violence in our schools, these stories never made the headlines. The triumph of the day was coming home unscathed. You realized quickly that no one was going to come rescue you or solve your problems. If you didn't want to get beaten up all the time, you taught yourself how to get out of fights, diffuse hostility, and de-escalate situations.

Every day was a dress rehearsal for me. You eventually figured out how to put on a mask to hide your fears, read body language, and portray a conciliatory demeanor. You learned to smile, disarm the fist, and talk yourself out of fights. Maybe this is what psychologists John Mayer and Peter Salovey spoke about when they developed the concept of emotional intelligence (EQ) in the early '90s as the new dominant trait for successful leaders. Daniel Goldman has since perpetuated the benefits of EQ, and the concept has spread pervasively in the business world in the form of programs and training in every business school and sector. I just wished that the concept of EQ was available in the '70s so we didn't have to wait for brilliant researchers to synthesize the emotional benefits in a manual for the world to consume. No, we learned it instinctively in order to survive the streets of Chinatown.

I used to think of my scar as a defective part of my life and would try to conceal that flaw with my sister's makeup foundation, but now I wear it like a badge of honor. The blistering pain from the stitches is long gone. Although time and age have blended my scar in with the rest of my wrinkles, it is now a reminder of how far I have come. My scar no longer weeps. In fact, it gave me the motivation I needed to make a better life for myself.

The Drudgery Walk

I continued to play basketball after school at Alpine throughout junior high, sometimes until dusk descended on me. After dinnertime, it was study and then sleep. Basketball was a respite from the gang fights throughout the day. It was my saving grace. By this time, all the hours spent playing basketball after school had honed my skills. I became one of the best young players on the playground, and I was always chosen first as the foundational piece that coaches built around at city-run basketball leagues. I was quick, could handle the ball, and score from just about every angle on the court. I felt terrific because all the coach's plays were run for me to score. When you have confidence, you attract people and doors open. Opposing coaches started noticing me and opportunities began to appear.

Coach Marty was my first mentor. He would pick me up from my house, take me to practice, and then treat me to McDonald's after each practice. We ended up winning every season and were competitive in inter-city tournaments as well. When you are poor, sometimes you feel like nothing is possible. Basketball changed my warped view and taught me what it is like to be a winner. When you win, you feel confident, and nothing is impossible. At this point for me, a day without basketball was a wasted day. I would manage to play basketball for a couple of hours every day, no matter how busy I was.

Eventually, I caught the eye of an opposing coach, Mr. Salcedo, who was also a PE coach at Nightingale. Coach Salcedo was a relentless advocate for disadvantaged kids, especially those from minority backgrounds. He recruited me and formed an all-star team to play against other schools. For three months each year, he would drive a bunch of us after school to compete in tournaments to keep us out of trouble. He was a great man. In three years, we only lost one game. My confidence grew so high at this point I felt like I was always wide open even when I was closely guarded. I was so thankful to Coach Salcedo. He gave me a purpose: an after-school basketball program that gave me confidence and kept us safe. He drove us around to basketball games and paid for all the expenses. It was a scary, frustrating, and exhausting six years since we'd arrived in America, but Coach Salcedo provided me with hope and optimism. This newfound confidence bled into other parts of my life as well.

At fifteen and a half, I started earning money from my first job as an assistant recreational aide for Chinatown Teen Post, now renamed the Chinatown Service Center. Since I knew Alpine like my own backyard, Coach Edmund hired me to check out equipment for the playground's patrons. It didn't pay much, but I felt like my life was turning around.

By tenth grade, I was pretty good at talking my way out of trouble. There were still plenty of fights, but it was nothing like Nightingale. The main targets were now the new immigrants who came after us, and unfortunately, they endured the same fate we did. They were recruited by gangs offering them a brotherhood, and they fought back against other gangs ferociously. Maybe it was a bit of battle fatigue, but I was so tired of the brawls that went on throughout the day. But with a more normal life, I was eager to realize the dream of getting into college.

In high school, I applied myself to schoolwork and was one of the top students in my graduating class. But I definitely spent more time playing basketball than I did studying, probably at a ratio of two to one. I felt terrible when I received a B grade but was not overly concerned about finishing as valedictorian or in the top ten like students do nowadays in high school. I also didn't go to any of the football games or post-win celebrations at Tommy's (a burger joint). It wasn't my cup of tea. I played basketball until late evening all year round.

During this time, I don't know how they did it, but my parents had saved enough money for a down payment to buy a house in Monterey Park, a place where the more acclimated Asian immigrants had chosen to cluster around and establish themselves. The move followed the path of Chinese immigrants from Chinatown to Monterey Park, representing a fortune change. My junior high years had been frantic and uncertain, and the relocation meant more stability, from blight to promise. The road ahead was looking even brighter for us.

My dad was now a chef at Don the Beachcomber, an upscale Chinese-fusion restaurant located in Marina del Rey that served pricey imitation Chinese food. I loved to visit him during off-hours because he would cook up a few specialty dishes for me. The restaurant manager and waiters treated me like family and would talk to me like an adult. My mom continued to work as a seamstress in Chinatown, and we had worked it out so that I could continue to play basketball at Belmont High School without having to transfer to a new school and start all over. I felt awful that my mom still had to work as a seamstress. But she was always optimistic and never complained. To ease the burden on her, my brother and I would share a car and pick her up from work after my basketball practice, and we would then drive home together.

Eventually, I excelled as a freshman on the high school sophomore basketball team as a prolific scorer. At the end of the basketball season, I was named Second Team All-League and was a shoo-in to play on the varsity basketball team the following year. But because of my showboating style, the varsity coach had me practice with the sophomore team to hone my leadership skills. I protested and defied the situation by not trying as hard during practices. I felt like I was being snubbed by the coach for a lack of leadership skills that I didn't comprehend to be valuable at the time (humility being one of them). To prove that I was more than prepared to play at the top level, my friend Wai and I challenged the varsity basketball players in a two-on-two, round-robin style pick-up game to prove that we belonged on their team. The winners would stay on until they lost. We never lost. They couldn't stop me. I was exhilarated. It made me feel validated that it was their loss not moving me up to varsity immediately. The informal game lasted hours and I completely lost track of time. When I realized how late it was, I left abruptly. I drove as fast as I could to pick up my mom at the factory, parked illegally, and ran inside. There were empty sewing machines, and it was eerily silent. The owner came out and told me that my mom had left an hour ago.

I jumped back into the car and drove up to Sunset Boulevard, hoping to intercept her. From a distance, I saw this diminutive person with an elongated shadow that made her look longer than she really was. She was carrying two plastic bags, one in each hand, and she was shifting the bags, trying to balance the weight distribution. She had her large purse draped over her body that functioned as a third bag with lighter items like zippers in it. It looked like she was doing a farmer's walk with twenty-pound dumbbells in each hand, sludging up the hill wearing a ten-pound jacket.

I pulled up next to her, got out of the car, took the bags from her, and opened the car door to let her in. She never asked me why I was late and proceeded to ask if I was hungry. In Chinese culture, this is how we express our love to each other. It didn't matter the time of day or whether you had just eaten, they wanted to make sure that we didn't starve. I told her no and that I had lost track of time. I asked her why she had two bags that day, and she said she was given an opportunity to earn some extra money. One bag had pants for her to sew seams together for twenty-five cents a pair, and in the other bag, she had zippers that she could get fourteen cents more by adding a zipper on each pair of pants. I had some idea that she was underpaid, but I didn't know what to say. I don't know how many zippers at fourteen cents each it took for her to put food on the table and pay for daily expenses, but my parents never questioned us when we asked them for money. I will never forget the unconditional sacrifices she made for us. She instilled in me a sense of resolve that has carried me through some trying times. The image of my mom clutching the flimsy handles of the brown paper bags in each hand just to bring in a week's worth of groceries will forever be engraved in my heart. Her grit and perseverance will never be forgotten.

The Silent Immigrants

Eventually, my parents saved up enough money to open a market in South Central Los Angeles. My mom and oldest brother would leave early in the morning to open the store, while my dad would go to a discount supermarket to pick up low inventory items. To have product variety, he would also pick up merchandise from Chinatown. The business was not a huge moneymaker, but it was enough to help subsidize the tuition for one of my brothers to attend medical school.

We were truly living the American dream. However, my family's market was consistently broken into in the middle of the night when police patrol was scarce. At 2 a.m. one morning, we received a call from the police informing us that they had caught seven criminals who broke into our store through the roof. They asked that we come down to the station to identify the merchandise that was found in the back of a station wagon. When we arrived at the police station, my parents whispered to me that they were the young men who came in every day to buy liquor, and frequently, my parents would give them free food and sodas. But my parents were afraid to say anything for fear of retaliation. Sensing our trepidation, the lieutenant told us to come back in a couple of days to identify the stolen goods and file charges if we wanted to.

For the next three days, glass bottles were hurled into the open glass doors every two to three hours. A couple of times, the shattered glass would graze my brother, cutting him in the arm. The shards of the broken pieces cut more than just skin; it marked the end of my parents' entrepreneurial dream. The gangsters got more and more aggressive each day, and finally just gathered in front of the store to harass customers, deterring them from coming in. Eventually, we succumbed to the pressure and closed the store. We never went back to file charges.

Although my parents capitulated to the aggression and kept silent, they never lost hope in the American dream. I made a mental contract with myself to always speak up, and under no circumstances, back down from criminals in these situations when I got older.

The rest of my high school years were relatively uneventful. After competing against more physically gifted basketball players from other inner-city schools like Crenshaw and Hamilton, I realized that I would not have a career in the NBA. With the ongoing conflict with the varsity coach, I made the painful decision to quit the basketball team.

With so much of my identity-forming years tied to basketball, I didn't know what to do in my spare time. I didn't share my friends' passion for community service. Wai and I started drifting apart when he began to hang out with the top students in the school. They had goals and wanted to change the world, and they naturally hung out with other students who shared similar passions and dreams. They avoided me because I was dragging them down. Without a close network of friends, I began loafing and wallowing in self-pity.

The White-Out

I waited a long time to apply for college because I didn't know what schools to apply to that would fit my interest. Ms. Crowell, my beloved health science teacher, took an interest in my future and volunteered to write a letter of recommendation for me. She was very popular and well-liked by students. One afternoon during recess, she searched me out, led me into her classroom, and shut the door. Without a smile on her face, she handed me college admission packages from UCLA and Cal State LA, her alma mater, and said she wanted the applications completed by the end of the week, which was five days before the actual deadline.

I didn't know what to write about, and seeing that I was experiencing brain fog, Ms. Crowell brought in the school's valedictorians, Raul and Alex, to help me generate ideas for my admission essays. They both recommended that I create a "fit" to match what colleges wanted to hear. Raul had applied to UCLA and wrote about giving back to his community as a doctor. Alex applied to USC and wrote about the underserved Asians in Chinatown who needed affordable medical services. Both essays were beautifully written and impactful. They had altruistic goals, and both went on to become doctors at their alma maters, respectively. I wanted to matter and have meaning in my life as they did. I emulated them and made up a story about my love of mathematics and how I would like to be a high school math teacher at inner-city schools. After sequestering myself for one week during nutrition and lunch, I finally completed the essays. Ms. Crowell had both Raul and Alex read them and they were both happy with the "fit" I fabricated. I was done.

When I got home, I reread my essay and was ready to sign it, send in the required fees, and be done with it. But knowing that my essays were riddled with fabricated dreams that I did not actually believe in or envision, I felt like I had to rewrite them. Suddenly, the poignant picture of my mom dredging up the hill in the scorching sun carrying a heavy bag in each hand burst into my mind. A wave of emotions came over me, and I could not stop crying. I was not good enough to play basketball professionally, I hated mathematics, I never wanted to be a schoolteacher, I had no passion for community service, and I had absolutely no idea what I wanted to do. I just didn't want to relive what my parents had gone through: working day and night day just to put food on the table. They had no voice in society because of a crippling language barrier. They were taken advantage of because they could not read and write in English.

I became angry and sobbed uncontrollably. The pent-up frustration and impatience of imagining something better and greater but instead having to endure the fear and pain made me bitter and furious. I was an imposter pretending to be someone I wasn't in my original essay because I thought

I had to play the game to get into college. But I just couldn't fake it anymore, I want to tell the world that we were misled into believing that there was a Gold Mountain here, but all we had were broken dreams. I was tired of living in a country that didn't accept me for who I was. I would rather be the exuberant gaper in a cricket competition in Hong Kong than a punching bag here in America. My parents wanted so much more for us, but I didn't think it was possible because of the challenging environment and constant terror.

I took my white-out and brushed the correction fluid all over my essay. But because of the unevenness of the watery substance, it left bumps and crust all over the paper like white sand. I opened a new bottle and applied a second layer of paint like an artist would, hoping that the unevenness of the white-out crust would be washed away by the next tide. It was not. The end result was a disaster that looked like a windstorm had displaced sand on the beach, leaving behind hilly and asymmetrical dunes. Instead of wasting more time, I just scribbled my name at the top of the crusted page and began writing over the patchy layers of white-out on the paper.

I wept silently as I rewrote my college essay. The story was about a kid who had big dreams of coming to America. He was the envy of all his classmates. But now, he was more than 7,000 air miles from his grandma and friends. In Hong Kong, he saw his parents regularly, but now they had to work all the time in menial jobs. The immigrant kid withstood the mocking and ridicule from strangers who didn't even know him but chose to inflict physical pain on him because he was a foreigner, physically weak, and poor. He endured the physical pain of punches and kicks and had a two-inch scar on this face to show for it. He hated America. It was a country he wanted to love but it didn't love him back. He was excited to be here, but the country did not embrace him. His experience was not the America he had dreamed about, the land of opportunity where everyone is treated equally. He missed home.

I didn't even proofread it. I just signed and mailed the application to UCLA. I had no expectations or future plans; I just wanted to find a job and make money. Therefore, I was ecstatic when I was accepted to UCLA! I even received enough grants and financial aid to get me through graduation. They also offered me a summer program to start taking classes and get me acclimated to the big university. But I declined because that summer, I found a job as an assistant math teacher (go figure) at an elementary school, and I wanted to make some money before I started college.

There were no YouTube college reaction videos, and I celebrated my college acceptance by skipping my graduation. It wasn't that big of a deal for me, and there was no time for immediate gratification. My anxiety waned and was replaced with a growing sense of optimism and confidence. Everything looked different that day. The sky looked a little bluer, the air smelled a little fresher, and I felt a little stronger. The future prize of college was ahead of me.

PART TWO
BEYOND CHINATOWN

*Our growth is only limited by
the size of our world.*

Best Friends

Sophomore Team As A Freshman

All League Second Team

Tae Kwon Do

The Gracie Brothers

My Idol

The Coolidge Boys-40 Years Later

4

BECOMING

The immigrant experience does not fit a template, and a decade of racial tension took a toll on me. I was physically beaten down and emotionally drained. For the last ten years of my life, I felt like a faceless immigrant living in a constant state of fear in a country that didn't truly accept me because of my skin color. Assimilating to America, surviving the mean streets of Chinatown, and living through the gang hostility in schools were probably the most trying years of my life. Even though it felt like we were always walking into headwinds, I believed that studying at one of the most recognizable and top universities in the world would allow me to finally swim with the current in the ebb and flow of life.

I now lived on the campus of arguably the perennial number one or two public university in the nation with breathtaking buildings and architecture, lots of open space, and boundless energy. UCLA made me feel like I was destined for greatness on the biggest stage of life, even though I didn't know what that meant or where that was. The conditions of growing up in Chinatown provided the motivation I needed to drive forward, and the possibility of earning a college degree gave me the hope to keep on dreaming. Perhaps the American nirvana that Hong Kongers dreamed about did exist, or maybe we just had to stop searching for the Gold Mountain and look elsewhere.

On my first day of school, I was in awe. I walked up the approximately 1,600 feet of the famed Bruin Walk, which in my mind was equivalent to Hollywood's Walk of Fame for stars. It was a concrete pathway paved with bricks sandwiched between dozens of tables from different ethnic groups, religious organizations, fraternities, and sororities. The scene reflected the rich tapestry of cultures in the world that we lived in, a community of people coming together to share their stories and achieve their dreams. Immediately, my horizon expanded across the globe.

Before UCLA, my world was microscopic, from Chinatown to the beach, a twenty-two-mile radius about the size of Hong Kong. In elementary school, I didn't stray far from what I was familiar or comfortable with. I was a passive participant who just wanted to belong and hang out with my group of friends that I had known since coming to America. In junior high, I was insecure, pretty much stayed in my lane, and goofed off with friends from elementary school.

Although I eventually became adept at de-escalating hostile situations and negotiating my way out of fights, I was very insecure and always put up a brave front. There was a natural hierarchy based on one's popularity in high school, starting with the athletes, cheerleaders, scholars, and at the end of the pecking order, the most recent immigrants. The latter was faceless, nameless, and anonymous. I was straddling between being a scholar and an athlete at the same time but did not reach top-tiered status in either arena. UCLA expanded my world through interacting with people from all walks of life. Each person had a different story, and we learned to get along and discovered our identities and values.

It is incredible how what is said in one domain can have a different meaning under a different setting. In junior high school, the dictum "See you after school" meant a fight was looming, and you had to get into a mental mindset to fight or talk yourself out of a fight. In high school, the phrase "Where you from" represented the challenge of a gang's superiority and dominance over you. You either defended yourself or walked away, capitulating to the challenge. In college, "See you after class" was an invitation to hang out with someone, and "Where you from" was a way to bridge commonality and share culture. The college experience gave me the confidence to reach out socially to strangers and acquaintances without the fear of rejection. For the first time in my life, I was unapologetically proud to be Asian.

My steps were light and peppy, reflecting my mood. Despite the intense competition at UCLA, I adapted well to the new environment. I did well in my freshman and sophomore years. The first year was about studying and surviving the rigorous structure of academic life at a big university, and at the same time, creating a network of friends that I could have fun with. I attended classes throughout the day, studied between classes, and did homework at night.

However, once I got into a cadence of campus life, I started spending a lot more time playing basketball and partying than I did studying. I played in intramural basketball leagues and every pick-up game against anyone who was willing. Again, through basketball, I made many friends. On weekends, I looked for parties and asked girls out on dates. The pattern repeated itself for the first two years, and notwithstanding all the partying and alcohol, my grades were decent. I didn't know what I was good at or what my passion was, all I wanted to do was eventually graduate, find a good job, and meet the hottest girl of my dreams.

Maybe it was because I was now more confident, I became very sociable and made friends easily and quickly. I particularly enjoyed striking up conversations with strangers on their commutes to school, mingling with friends of friends at parties, and introducing myself to people on the outskirts of my social circles. Most people tend to reserve the most meaningful connections of their day for their closest friends, but I genuinely felt an immense degree of satisfaction after an interaction with a stranger as though I had just spoken to a close friend. I enjoyed uncovering surprising tidbits about a modest person on the bus who turned out to be an accomplished dancer, or an unassuming surfer whose father ran a Fortune 30 company (both true stories). These chance encounters and interactions were always pleasant and added texture to my day. Throughout my college years, I felt a sense of freedom but without the responsibilities of true adulthood. The college experience shaped my worldview. It was a coming of age.

5

THE COOLIDGE HOUSE

After my freshman and sophomore years living in the dorms, I decided to move in with five guys I had met at random parties. We moved into a house on Coolidge Street that we astutely named the Coolidge House. While casual acquaintances are typically friendships of utility, this particular group of guys blossomed into my closest circle of friends. We were bound not by genetics or blood but by the joy we shared in each other's lives. We chose to grow up under the same roof and stood beside each other through thick and thin. Our friendships were connected by loyalty, and whether in good or bad times, they were the ones who showed up when it mattered most. They accepted me whether I was miserable, happy, or moody. They thought I was perfect even when I was broken and imperfect. They were my family away from home.

These special friendships formed the backbone of trust and family beyond the college years. Graduating from

UCLA, immersing myself in the whole college experience, and developing these lifelong friendships were truly some of the most significant turning points in my life. Together we felt like we could conquer the world, yet individually we were unique and special. They taught me the values of kindness, compassion, generosity, independence, risk-taking, empathy, and loyalty. After we graduated from college, we pursued our own career paths, and with shifting priorities, distance, and time, our friendships slowly dwindled. But the bond and fond memories we shared will always remain in my heart. These were their gifts to me.

Gus

Gus was a graduate student at UCLA, a bright and thoughtful fellow with a penchant for fine wine. I can't remember how we met, but it was probably through a friend of a friend at a party or on the basketball court. Gus came from an extremely well-to-do family with both parents having PhDs. We got along great and decided to room together in my junior year along with two other friends.

Gus was the parent and de facto head of the Coolidge House. He shopped for groceries, cooked, and divided up the expenses every month. My junior and senior years were academically challenging. The concepts in the core electrical engineering classes were hard to grasp and getting an A in any subject felt like winning the Pulitzer Prize for me. There were just so many smarter and more motivated students than me. I remembered a sixteen-year-old student sitting in the front row of a computer class peppering the professor with questions that I couldn't even comprehend. The stress of countless sleepless nights spent studying wore me down physically and made me sick repeatedly. My perpetual illness caused me to miss many classes, but thank God for lecture notes and friends, because I was barely keeping up. Fortunately, UCLA offered tutoring programs to make sure I was successful, and between tutors, intelligent friends, lecture notes, and sleepless nights, I survived.

When I was bedridden, it was Gus who took care of me. While all the other roommates avoided me, he would make me chicken soup, go to the drugstore to get Tylenol, and check up on me to make sure I was all right. It was emotionally the best chicken soup I ever had because it was the highest expression of friendship and fellowship I have ever experienced.

When Gus found out that I had never seen snow, he organized a weekend trip to Tahoe with some close friends so I could experience my first ski excursion. After getting nauseated from the two-hour winding drive, we all settled in and had a night of fun drinking beer and playing games. The next day, we all met up on the ski slopes and ran into friends that we partied with often. That was the first time I have ever been on a ski slope and seen so much snow.

Dying to show them that skiing was as easy as playing basketball, I hopped on a ski lift and confidently waved at my friends. However, after spending the next twenty minutes falling and rolling down a bunny slope, I could not even stand still without slipping or tumbling. Those twenty minutes felt like twenty hours. While all my friends started dispersing to what they called a Black Diamond run, I was left to fend for myself on the dreaded bunny slope. Seeing that I was helpless, Gus stayed with me, taught me how to snowplow, and spent the next three hours with me until I was comfortable enough to have fun on my own. After he made sure I was self-sufficient, he left to look for the others.

While on my own, I sprained my left knee and quit in frustration. At this point, my denim jeans and oversized sweatshirt were soaking wet, and I was shivering trying to dry up. That's when I noticed that I was the only one of all my friends without ski pants and a jacket. I didn't even know they had special clothing for skiers. An hour later, Gus found me shivering in a café and gave me his ski jacket. He said, "I will take you back to the cabin, and then I will come back to pick up the others." I didn't want to play the tough guy anymore and accepted his offer. I was so glad to be back in the cabin with the amenities of a bed and TV. I didn't go back on the ski slope the rest of the trip, and today, I still don't miss it. But I miss Gus. He now lives in Silicon Valley with his wife and two sons, a six hour drive from Los Angeles. I will forever remember his kindness and compassion.

Jack

Jack was Gus's best friend. Jack had graduated from UCLA and was working for one of the largest Japanese car makers in the world. He also came from a well-to-do family, but he never acted materialistic or pompous because of his wealth; in fact, he was quite down to earth. We bonded by spending hours together at Tower Records and grabbing dinner afterward.

Jack knew that I didn't have much money and would always pay for my meal when just the two of us went out to eat together. He was game for just about anything. Jack introduced me to the Nissan 300 ZX and would let me drive his whenever I wanted. He never asked me for gas money or inspected the car for scratches or damages after I borrowed it. He only cared how my night went and what I thought of the car's performance. His influence was the reason I bought the same car after I landed my first job.

When I was laid off from my first job, I didn't tweet it like today's tech-savvy millennials would, I stopped by the Coolidge House to drink with my former roomies. When I went inside the house, only Jack was there. When I told him I was laid off from my job, he didn't console me or give me any words of wisdom, he simply took me out to a sushi bar and got me drunk on sake. Jack now lives in Texas with his wife and daughter, and other than the annual Christmas card updates, we didn't stay in touch. But I reminisce about our time together fondly.

Alan

My third roommate, Alan, whom I had shared a bedroom with, was kind of quiet and mostly kept to himself. He didn't share his personal life much and was more of an observer at parties. We were the most similar from a social-economic perspective because we both depended on using Pell Grants and other financial aid and loans to survive the costs of college. Since we were not in the position to pay for alcohol and snacks every weekend for parties, we would skip meals so we could contribute our share of the party expenses.

Still unable to shake off the virus and bacteria that had plagued me all my life, I was thankful that he tolerated my germ-spreading ways. Alan and his wife, Flo, now reside in Temecula, California with their growing family of five. We actively stay in touch on Facebook and in-person on special occasions.

Gus, Jack, and Alan were the perfect roomies. We would take turns cooking and do our chores until one evening, I microwaved the pork chops too long and was promptly relieved of all future cooking duties. They now believe that it was my way of getting out of cooking responsibilities and we still laugh about it. We would play hoops two to three times a week at Pauley Pavilion and through these impromptu games, we made so many lasting friendships. Friends we met would invite us to parties, and our social network of friends continued to grow exponentially. If there were no parties that weekend, we would throw our own parties. Before long, Coolidge House became the central party house. Friends would bring friends, and we became the place that friends would start talking about on Thursday nights. Andy and Jack would pay for just about all the snacks and alcohol and never asked me for reimbursements. My contribution was to invite friends to the parties. The weekend parties went on for two years. I would study Monday through Thursday, party on Fridays and Saturdays, and then recover on Sundays. Life was simple and fun. Our little family of four eventually burgeoned to six.

Tai

Tai was from New York and graduated with a degree in computer science from Stonybrook. He worked for one of the largest aerospace companies in the world but didn't like his job. He always had one foot out the door while he was working. During one of the pick-up basketball games at Pauley, we had accidentally left photos of a party that we hosted the weekend before. He found these pictures at the gym and delivered them to us. We thanked him and invited him in for a drink, and before he left, he asked if we were looking for another roommate. Seeing that he had a nice car and was already out of school and working, we told him we would call him back. That night, we unanimously agreed that having another roommate would lower the rent payment and lessen the burden of these party expenses.

This guy knew how to live life. He drove a white spiffed-up Trans Am, had five pairs of brand-name tennis shoes, and ate out quite a bit. On weekends, Tai would work nights at a nightclub by the beach, and he would let us in for free. Tai was embarking on a real estate career part-time while he was working as a software engineer. He began investing and rehabbing undervalued properties and then taking out equity from the increased value to invest in more properties. Eventually, he overcame the "what if" indecision, left his job at the aerospace company, and went into real estate full time. He went through some rough patches during the real estate downturn, but persevered and became financially independent at a very young age. Tai went outside of his comfort zone and dealt with the uncertainty that goes along with taking risks. We became best friends, and he was a groomsman at my wedding. His wife, Jenny, also became my wife's best friend, and we often traveled together on vacations.

Norm

Norm is still one of the most genuine and empathetic people I have ever met. Norm spent so much time at the Coolidge House that when he asked if we needed another roommate, we didn't hesitate at all. There was a loft in the garage, and he didn't mind sleeping there. He always made sure everyone had a good time at parties and that no one was neglected.

I will never forget the time when he stuffed his finger in my mouth and tickled my throat to help me vomit when I was drunk. It wasn't pretty, and to most people, it was probably grotesque. But to me, that was the epitome of friendship. It was one thing to harbor a sense of empathy and another to put it into action. His sense of empathy was personified in this selfless act.

Another time, when I got sick during my first business trip in Boston, Norm and his best friend Marshall sent me a care package of homemade cookies to my hotel. I remembered tearing up when I first opened the boxes. The cookies worked like antibiotics and made me feel better immediately. They made me feel closer to home even though I was far away, cooped up in a hotel with torrential rain and twenty-degree Fahrenheit weather outside.

Norm was a groomsman in my wedding party. Norm and his wife, Jill, reside in Cerritos with their daughter and son.

Roxanne

Even though she didn't physically live with us, I would be remiss if I didn't include Roxanne as one of my best friends. Roxanne was an honorary roommate, and her frequent visits to the Coolidge House made us cool. She was the best friend whom I trusted and confided in during my college years.

Roxanne was there for every one of the weak moments of my college life. When my heart was broken, she was there to put the pieces back together. When I needed confidence, she told me how lucky the girls were to have me or how the next exam would be easier. When I was sick, she took care of me. When we went out partying, she kept an eye on me to make sure I didn't get in trouble. When I needed a friend, she always listened without judgment. I could mess up, and she still loved me.

That was my inner circle. We took care of each other and shared our fears and dreams uninhibitedly. While my birth family was linked by blood and DNA, my college family was bonded by adult experiences that included struggles, disappointments, and triumphs. We uplifted each other through all the broken hearts, tried to figure out our identities, and navigated life the best we could.

PART THREE
THE THANKSGIVING MIRACLE

*Being a dad is the greatest honor of my life.
Watching him grow up gave me the utmost joy,
and the man he is today continues to fill me
with ultimate pride.*

Catch of the Day

My Last First Date

Falling in Love

The Thanksgiving Miracle

Siesta

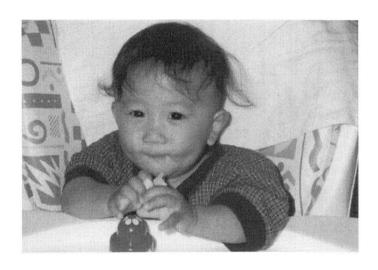

Happy Boy

Mommy and Me

The Unbreakable Bond

We Are Family

6

CATCH OF THE DAY

After graduation, I was focused on building a career, moved back home to save money to buy a house, and became a little disconnected from my friends. By this time, Norm had a girlfriend and was off the market, and all my friends were either paired up or had someone they were courting. It was the week before Halloween, and there were no parties that I had heard about or had been invited to attend. I called Norm and asked what he was doing for Halloween, and he informed me that the group had planned a party in Big Bear and was surprised I didn't know about it. I was embarrassed and told him that no one had invited me. He said to call Gus and Jack, who were planning the party. I called them, and they jokingly said since the primary activity was going to be fishing, and knowing that I was allergic to patience, they didn't want to bore me with a whole weekend of trawling. But before we hung up, they gave me an open invitation.

Still debating whether or not I wanted to go, I called Norm and asked who else would be there besides the old gang. Nonchalantly, he said it was pretty much everyone I knew. Just when I was ready to tell him I would pass, he said, "Wait, have you met Cathy? She also graduated from UCLA, and she was brought into the group by a mutual friend. She has been going dancing and partying with the group for about a year now." He said since he hadn't seen me in a while, he just wanted to be sure. I asked," Do you have a picture of her?" He said, "I have a group picture with her in it."

That night I drove to his house to take a look at the picture. Bam! Wow! Holy cow! The theme song of Batman started playing in my head. I told Norm that I had seen her on the UCLA campus in passing but never talked to her. I always thought this girl was attractive. She looked ethnically ambiguous. Was she Asian? Hispanic? European? All three? Immediately, I volunteered to pick up a friend who had to work late to drive up to Big Bear for the fishing.

We arrived just before dinner. I spotted Cathy in the crowd instantly. Her beauty was breathtaking. Instantly, my heart went into free fall. She was tall and slender, had smooth marble skin and big piercing eyes that sparkled. Her pearly white teeth would shine when she laughed. She was effortlessly beautiful and exuded an impeccable fashion sense and style with her casual yellow sweatpants, a white sweatshirt underneath a turquoise-blue oversized unbuttoned shirt. Time stood still. All my senses were heightened at that moment. That was the first time I had felt intoxicated without any alcohol.

After dinner, the large group broke out into smaller groups with different activities. Cathy was with a group of four playing board games with a card game going on next to her. Since poker was one of my favorite pastimes (along with mixed martial arts), I strategically joined the card game and took a seat on the floor directly behind her. Every minute or so, I would turn to talk to her. She was a great conversationalist and laughed at all my jokes.

Finally, I turned to her and asked her if it was okay for me to lean back against her back, and she didn't object. We held each other up with our backs supporting each other, and at that moment, an air bubble formed over us filled with chocolate and ice cream, her favorite foods. She had everything that I was looking for: beauty, brains, personality, and more beauty. We intermittently talked between games, and I found out that she also graduated from UCLA and was working for a community service organization and on her teaching credentials at the same time.

When the games ended, we all changed into our Halloween costumes, and since I was only there to meet her, I didn't bring one. She dressed up as Dorothy from *The Wizard of Oz*, and I was completely smitten by her beauty, secretly hoping that she didn't have to search for home anymore because I had been waiting here for her my whole life. I told her I did some palm reading and offered to read her fortune. She opened her hands, and after an intense minute staring at the palmar flexion creases on her palm, I told her it had EE written all over it. She asked me what EE meant, and I told her Ed Eng, my initials. She laughed and playfully slapped my arm. I was utterly infatuated with her by this time.

The next day, I did something I have never done before—I became a pseudo fisherman. While everyone marveled at the tranquility of the lake and grandeur of the mountain backdrop, I was more captivated by her natural beauty. Her simple attire of sweatpants and oversized jacket just added to her exquisiteness. The quote "beauty in simplicity" came to life for me that day. Before we said goodbye to this breathtaking getaway, we exchanged phone numbers.

Our first date was a three-hour marathon dinner at a Chinese restaurant. I ordered a seven-course meal to impress her, and I ended up being more impressed with her appetite. She also had no problem taking the leftovers home. The conversation ended when the waiters started flicking the lights on and off, hinting that the restaurant was closing. We looked around, and there was no one left except for us.

After our first date, I canceled the rest of my dates for the month. I just wanted to spend as much time with her as possible. By the end of the week, I knew I didn't want to go on another first date with anyone else again. I also began making mixed tapes of romantic songs of my favorite artists, which included, of course, the Bee Gees. In my mind, that was an integral part of courtship, and there was no more unambiguous indication of my affection than a carefully crafted mix of melodies strung together on a cassette tape.

For the next three years, we went to concerts, clubs, movies, dinners, beaches, or just stayed in and talked. After a three-year courtship, with a few fits and starts, we were married. We were both just starting in our careers without a care in the world. She had found her calling as a schoolteacher, and I was trying to climb the corporate ladder as an engineer.

I will forever be indebted to Norm for letting me know about Big Bear, where I caught the biggest fish of my life.

7

THE PERUVIAN RUG

The only thing I can say with 100 percent certainty is that we wanted to be parents. We are both from large families, so jokingly, we would negotiate how many kids we wanted to have and eventually settled on three or four. However, after five years of frustration trying to conceive unsuccessfully, and several health checks to look for defects in our internal systems, doctors did not find anything that would prevent us from having children. While being constantly reminded of our infertility condition from family and friends, I became bitter and desperate to have a family of our own, especially when watching how remarkable she was with our friends' kids. Throughout the journey, we remained optimistic despite living in a continuous state of fluctuating despair and hope.

Perhaps we could still live a fulfilled life without children. We could get another dog, volunteer, or be mentors to other sons and daughters. In my mind, I had to practice embracing a lonely vision of our future together because it was less painful to accept that than to hold out for something more. In my heart, though, there remained an emptiness and burning desire to have a family of greater than two.

Every weekend we would go to swap meets to browse but never bought anything. We would stop by this vendor who sold Peruvian rugs and marvel at the colorful geometric patterns woven in a way that was so aesthetically calming. Maybe it was the vibrant range of textile designs that reflected a unique heritage, or perhaps the richness of the stories behind each one. Nevertheless, it gave us a routine to help us not focus on the psychological trauma of infertility. But deep down, I was trying to adjust to a significant shift in life's expectations.

Finally, I accepted a managerial position with the Department of Water and Power (DWP) in Las Vegas to divert attention from my obsession of trying to have kids. Irrespective of the physical distance between us, we never missed a weekend of seeing each other. Every Friday afternoon, I would drive home to LA and then leave on Sunday nights after dinner. Then on a routine weekend, I got the most life-changing news of my life—Cathy was pregnant! After five futile years of trying unsuccessfully to conceive, by way of the miraculous science of artificial insemination, we were going to be parents!

I became a father midway through my MBA journey at Pepperdine University. I felt that we became whole. Immediately, my son Brandon became my highest priority. I would carry Brandon in one arm and sing Bee Gees songs to him while typing my papers with my free hand. When I got tired, I would put him in the rocking car seat and position him facing me, and occasionally watched him swatting the toys that hung on the seat handle. During study breaks, I would take him out of his seat, tickle him, and talk to him as if he understood me. That was my favorite pastime, and I would never trade that time for the world. At bedtime, I would make up fictitious stories with superhero characters since I wasn't familiar with American bedtime stories.

I was protective, doting, and engaged in all aspects of his life. I attended all his scheduled exams and frowned upon doctors who made him cry during quotidian checkups. I scolded one of the intern residents because he needed several attempts to perform a spinal tap which caused Brandon to endure unnecessary pain. I believe a father's highest responsibility is that of a protector and provider like my father was. Since I had made a promise never to let my kid get bullied like I was, I began training in martial arts long before Brandon was born. I guess it was to make up for my history of losing fights growing up. I quickly excelled in Taekwondo, and as a white belt, I more than held my own sparring with the black belts. After receiving my blue belt, I was already beating most of the black belts in the dojo, and no one wanted to spar with me. I later found out that other students felt that I was too aggressive. In my mind, I was willing to take punches and kicks as long as I could reciprocate at two or three times the force.

I continued to gain confidence, and, on a whim, I drove down to Torrance to test my skills against the famed Gracie family with their brand of BJJ of self-defense. In absolute defeat, I became a lifelong student and practitioner of this amazing art. In addition to spending countless hours on the mat, I also dabbled in Muay Thai for three years in a gym operated by a champion kickboxer. Although I was still playing basketball at a high level in various Asian leagues, martial arts eventually became my passion.

When Brandon turned three, we believed we had enough love to have siblings for him, but after two years of fruitless efforts, we started IVF treatment. In the third and final attempt, we were pregnant with a baby. But the triumph only lasted eighty-five days, we suffered a devastating miscarriage and never made it past the third trimester. The loss left a gaping hole in my heart, but we took comfort in the fact that we had Brandon. Maybe God wanted us to share our pain and hurt to produce something of greater value later.

In 2003, I ran into an old high school friend known for his fanatical admiration of Bruce Lee. A casual conversation turned into his revelation of struggles with infertility. He told me he had pretty much given up on having children of his own. At that moment, I felt his pain of feeling inadequate and unfulfilled, and I shared with him that we had pretty much given up as well, but the last artificial insemination attempt gave us Brandon. A year later, my friend called me out of the blue and told me that they were pregnant with a baby girl. I was overjoyed. He thanked me for giving him hope. Today, he has three beautiful kids.

With our hands full with Brandon, we never went back to the swap meet again, but each time I see a Peruvian rug, I am reminded to not give up hope in the most dire circumstances.

8

THE UNBREAKABLE BOND

Brandon must have inherited my sickly DNA because growing up, he was diagnosed with asthma, eczema, and various food allergies. Like me, Brandon was always one of the smallest and skinniest kids at his grade level. His small stature limited his aggressiveness in sports early on and throughout his elementary and middle school years. I knew his small stature would eventually invite bullies, so I became overtly visible at school to send messages to potential brutes and their fathers that no one would harass him. As a father, I just want people to treat my son the same when I was not there.

During an intense group discussion in one of my MBA classes, I received a frantic phone call from Cathy that she was taking Brandon, who was three months old at the time, to the hospital since his fever would not subside. She had called his pediatrician, who said to bring him in immediately to make sure the condition didn't develop into meningitis. My heart sank, and without packing my books or telling anyone why I was leaving, I just took off with nothing other than my car key.

As soon as Brandon saw me, he started crying and reached his hands out to me as if he was telling me to protect him. I frantically ran toward him, held him in my arms, and restlessly caressed his back. In my most soothing voice, I told him, "Daddy is here, and I will never let anything happen to you." On the way home, Cathy told me that the test involved drawing marrow from his back, and the resident doctor took three attempts to finally draw a suitable sample from Brandon. I was so upset but was grateful that at least he was going home. I was also glad that Cathy told me after the fact because I would have been upset and created an unwarranted scene. The next day, I called my professor and friends to explain what had happened, and they told me, "Next time, just give him Tylenol."

Because I knew from my experiences that Brandon's diminutive size would become the target of aggressive hooligans, I enrolled him in sports to improve his physical strength. In La Mirada, where we lived as a family, sports played a pivotal role in the community. Leagues were available for just about every sport and age group. Like other neighborhood kids, at seven years old, Brandon started playing baseball, soccer, and basketball. He didn't excel in baseball, and as he described it, "I don't see the point in bigger and stronger boys throwing rocks at me. What fun is that!" He also didn't get many opportunities during practice since all the attention went to the coach's kids and the good players. It wasn't until he played for Coach Ray that I felt he got the attention that all kids should get. Ray and his wife were active in VIP sports, leagues dedicated to special-needs youths. He never saw Brandon as a liability but just another kid who could excel like anyone else if given a chance. After games, Ray would point out all the positive things each kid did well during the game. He spent extra time with Brandon and made sure he got as many practice hits as everyone else. I will forever be grateful for how he advocated for Brandon.

Brandon played baseball for one season and quit. He was quick and excelled in soccer and would outrun everyone else to the ball and then kick it into the goal. He was used exclusively as a defender, but somehow, he played on a championship team that went to the regional playoffs as the leading scorer. He was exciting to watch, and I made it a point never to miss a game or practice. But life happens, and I had to miss one of his games because I couldn't get out of an important business trip. Cathy had me on the phone during the last two minutes of the game, and he ended up kicking in the winning goal. I was so disappointed that I didn't see this epic moment, but I felt better when he called me to tell me that he scored the winning goal. I told him I was sorry I wasn't there, and he simply said, "No big deal, Dad, you are always here." I cried that night because his maturity and understanding deeply touched me. I promised I would never miss another game, and I never did. Eventually, Brandon was burned out from the incessant practices and weekend travels under the scorching sun with sidewalks hot enough to cook an egg.

One weekend, as I was cleaning out the garage, Brandon saw a box full of basketball trophies and asked me how long I had to play to accumulate all those awards. I told him that they were accrued through a lifetime of playing in various leagues, but I started playing competitively in seventh grade as a safe haven from all the gang activities. I gave him a detailed account behind each trophy, and after a couple of hours of bonding, he said, "I want to give basketball a try."

I didn't want anyone to coach Brandon because I understood basketball. I ended up coaching him until he got into high school. He flourished very quickly and was the centerpiece of all the teams I coached, and together, we won at every level, in every league we played. His biggest test came during the summer before high school in a competitive National Junior Basketball (NJB) league. Assembling teams in NJB was similar to that of the NBA draft, coaches were recruiting behind the scenes, and some parents would only allow their kids to play for a particular coach. Being a rookie coach, I didn't know who the talented kids were, but I didn't care since I only wanted to coach my son and ended up with a team of misfits that no one wanted. We didn't have the best players, and the team was built around the most undersized point guard in the league and an introverted workman-like center.

I was a fiery coach during the games but a calm mentor after the game just like Coach Ray was in baseball and soccer when he coached Brandon. The transcendental formula of choosing to see the best in people and advocating for them became the tenets of my management philosophy later in life as well. I told every kid what their positives were and how we could improve as a team. We went 9-1 the entire season. The parents started believing in their kids and the potential of the team. We exceeded the expectations of the league by making it to the national finals but eventually lost to a better and more athletic team. It was then on to the All-Star selection and intercity playoffs featuring the best talents from participating cities.

Brandon was the top vote-getter for the All-Star team as polled by his peers in the league. I was by default the All-Star coach because we had the the best win-loss record. We made it all the way to the national semifinals and lost to a more talented team. The following year, he starred on the freshman high school team as their point guard. He wasn't a big scorer but definitely the leader of the team, and they won a majority of their games.

In his sophomore year, Brandon had a great start and stood out with his all-around game: precision passing, defense, and scoring. However, when the team hit a rough skid and started losing, he was relegated to coming off the bench because the coach said he wanted more athleticism at the point guard position. The change didn't work, and the team continued to lose while Brandon was further demoted to the third guard off the bench.

In a rare moment when Brandon got to play, amid a scramble that ended up with an opposing player headed for an uncontested layup, he hustled back on defense, poked the ball away, and fell out of bounds trying to save the ball. While all his teammates were still just watching from the offensive side of the court, the other team's players picked up the loose ball and scored easily. Angrily, the coach called a timeout, got in Brandon's face, started yelling at him on his way to the bench, and replaced him when live action resumed. I lost it! It was a coach's prerogative to bench him whenever he wants, but it was not acceptable for him to disrespect my son in public when he gave it his best.

I impatiently waited for the coaches after the game to confront them about my observations. With my heart beating through my t-shirt, muscles tensing up visibly, and veins sticking out of my arms, I contentiously told the head coach how unfair he was. I was not going to let anyone bully my son, even if it was the coach. I don't know what would have happened if the coach had talked back to me at that moment. Luckily, he acted more like an adult than I did and refused to engage with me. But my temper flared even more with the silent response, and I became emotional and combative. Finally, the assistant coach separated us and escorted the head coach to his car.

I immediately called the varsity coach, expressed my frustration, and asked for a resolution. At the meeting, Brandon's coach apologized but said that he saw the play differently. I strung together a couple of unprintable words and told all the coaches that they could do what they wanted with Brandon's playing time, but they were not permitted to ever disrespect him in public again.

Even though the coach did not yell at him anymore, his body language and head shaking told a different story. He began second-guessing every decision Brandon made on the court. However, with or without Brandon playing, the team continued to lose with no end in sight. It was apparent that the game was no longer fun for Brandon. He stopped taking risks and was afraid to make mistakes for fear of being benched with the already little time he was getting. But the negative environment had already sucked the passion out of him, and I instinctively knew it was just a matter of time before he would move on from playing basketball competitively.

After the entire summer of enduring the coach's resentment and wrath, Brandon was put in a position to play when both the starting and reserve guards were out with injuries. With the team depleted, the coach told Brandon, "It is all you, Brandon, this is your chance to show what you can do." He ended up having one of the best statistical games he ever played: eighteen points and ten assists. The rest of the team also stepped up and played their best game ever. It was pretty obvious what they needed was Brandon's leadership and all the intangible things that he brings: staying calm under pressure, making that extra pass to an open shooter, and encouraging a teammate when he misses a wide-open layup. Brandon never relinquished his spot again after that game, and the team was back on the winning track. They finished the regular season 8-2, and Brandon started every game. But the season had taken an emotional toll on him, and viscerally, I was aware that his enjoyment for basketball had waned, and it was a matter of time before he fell out of love with the game.

The following year, Brandon was promoted to varsity as a junior. He had a grueling schedule, took all AP classes, played on the varsity basketball team, and was tied for valedictorian honors. Every day, there was mandatory weightlifting after basketball practice, and by the time he got home, it was usually around 7 p.m. After a quick dinner, he would stay up until 2 a.m. to finish his homework. Eventually, Brandon's asthma got worse, and he started getting sick. But to prove his commitment, he continued to play through his sickness. One Saturday, after he had left for practice, I noticed that he had left his asthma inhaler at home and called him immediately. Since he had just driven off, he decided to come back to pick up the inhaler instead of having me deliver it to him. The short interruption caused him to be one minute late to practice, and as a punishment for the delay, he was locked out of the gym for half an hour before rejoining the team for practice.

Three days later, he came to me and said he wanted to quit basketball. I asked him why and he said, "Coming off the bench as the eleventh player on a twelve-man team and spending up to four or five hours a day practicing is not the best use of my time." Without saying a word, we just hugged, and after a prolonged silence, I told him that we would support whatever he chose to do. I had to learn to see the world through Brandon's eyes. Despite our best intentions, as parents, sometimes what we want for our kids do not align with what they want. The general myth that quitting is never the right thing to do is just nonsense to me. I know that the perception of quitting a sport is sometimes vilified as the mark of failure and a sign of weakness, but I believe talent and perseverance will only get you so far without genuine passion. There is a time to persevere and a time to let go, and Brandon's courage and ability to know the difference was one of his greatest attributes. I admired him for his decision.

After a couple of weeks of no basketball, I could already feel his energy level bouncing back from the extra four hours of no more obligatory weightlifting and basketball practices. One evening after dinner, he just played his drums for three straight hours. Other than the occasional eardrum spasm in our tensor tympani muscles, the live concert was beautiful because he was completely immersed in the extra time gained to explore his passion. When Brandon was young, Cathy had enrolled him in guitar, drums, cooking, and art lessons to stimulate the creative right hemisphere of his brain. He didn't play video games like all his friends but engulfed himself in the Guitar Hero drum set and progressed to the most complex beats quickly. To nurture what we perceived as a natural talent, we enrolled him in drum lessons and bought him a professional drum set equipped with stands, cymbals, toms, and other accessories.

After he quit basketball, he got together with some friends, formed a band, and played at carnivals and community events. Other than enduring the noise from their twice-a-week practices at our house, they sounded great as a garage band. They even wrote an original song that took second place in a Battle of the Bands community concert. Their prize was three hours of recording time in an actual studio. The original song they recorded was put on iTunes and downloaded fifty-six times.

Brandon also took up bodybuilding to stay in shape, and in a very short time, he had transformed his once slim physique to one packed with rippling muscles. He grew to love contact sports and was no longer the sickly kid he once was. He was driven and had a laser-focus like no other kids I had ever seen. In preparation for his college years, I enrolled him in BJJ lessons for self-defense, and once again, he excelled and became proficient at a rapid pace.

Even with a new body to flaunt and supreme confidence, the rigor of taking all AP classes still took an emotional toll on Brandon. He said he did it just to bolster his chances of getting into his dream college, but the extreme stress that came with such a taxing schedule was not worth it. The hard work eventually paid off and Brandon became the co-valedictorian of his high school. In his valedictorian speech, he thanked his grandparents for their sacrifices, and he publicly made a promise never to squander the opportunity they had given him.

Brandon's college years were spectacular. He interviewed and was selected by a prestigious consulting club on campus in his freshman year, interned for a colossal entertainment company the summer before his sophomore year, and consulted for several tech companies throughout the school year. He was offered a job as a business analyst by Amazon before starting his junior year and went on to graduate in three years. After a year, he left Amazon to work as a data manager at a mature startup company, followed by executive roles for a small startup music company and a nascent startup tech company. Eventually he founded his own digital marketing agency. He has developed into a purposeful young man with confidence, ambition, and, most of all, grit.

I watched when Brandon first learned to turn over. I was there when he took his first steps. I sang to him and cradled him to sleep when he was colicky. I carried and comforted him when he was sick. I attended all his games and practices except for one. I held his bike and ran with him side by side until he was secure enough to ride off on his own. I held and consoled him when he missed shots at the end of basketball games. I hugged him tight when his heart was broken. I listened to him as he navigated corporate politics and structure.

For me, there is no bigger joy in life than being a dad. Through all the pains and triumphs, I can unequivocally pronounce to the world that fatherhood will always be my most significant privilege in life. It was only after I became a dad that I truly embraced the adage "What are you willing to die for?" Although Chinese culture makes it hard to say "I love you" or express love for people you are close to, I am glad we can say it freely to each other. I love you, son!

PART FOUR
THE LOS ANGELES TIMES

Do not label any job a "dream job" because once you do, you become complacent, avoid taking risks, and lose the edge of what got you there in the first place.

The Metal Rice Bowl

Los Angeles Times

KATHRYN M. DOWNING
Publisher, President and Chief Executive Officer

MICHAEL PARKS
Editor and Executive Vice President

JOHN ARTHUR
Managing Editor, Regional Editions

JOHN P. LINDSAY
Managing Editor, Features

KAREN WADA
Managing Editor, Projects

LEO C. WOLINSKY
Managing Editor, News

FRANK DEL OLMO
Associate Editor

NARDA ZACCHINO
Associate Editor and Vice President

LEAH M. GENTRY
Editorial Director, New Media

JANET CLAYTON
Editor of the Editorial Pages and Vice President

ELIZABETH V. DREWRY
Senior Vice President, Human Resources

JAMES D. HELIN
Senior Vice President, Chief Marketing Officer

BONNIE G. HILL
Senior Vice President, Communications and Public Affairs

JUDITH S. KALLET
Senior Vice President and Chief Information Officer

MARK H. KURTICH
Senior Vice President, Operations

ROBERT G. MAGNUSON
Senior Vice President, Regions

JOHN C. MCKEON
Senior Vice President, Advertising

RICHARD W. STANTON
Senior Vice President and Chief Operations Officer

JULIE K. XANDERS
Senior Vice President, General Counsel

VICE PRESIDENTS
CHRIS K. AVETISIAN
BEVERLY A. DREHER
EDWARD ENG
KARLENE GOLLER
THOMAS W. KELLY
RENÉE E. LABRAN
KIM M. LA FRANCE
STEVEN U. LEE
RAYMOND MCCUTCHEON
ROGER OGLESBY
CAROL PERRUSO
DENNIS A. SHIRLEY
JULIA C. WILSON

HARRISON GRAY OTIS, *Publisher,* 1882-1917
HARRY CHANDLER, *Publisher,* 1917-1944
NORMAN CHANDLER, *Publisher,* 1944-1960
OTIS CHANDLER, *Publisher,* 1960-1980
TOM JOHNSON, *Publisher,* 1980-1989
DAVID LAVENTHOL, *Publisher,* 1989-1994
RICHARD SCHLOSBERG III, *Publisher,* 1994-1997
MARK H. WILLES, *Publisher,* 1997-1999

Published by The Times Mirror Company
MARK H. WILLES
Chairman, President and CEO

The Masthead

The Executive

Free Time

9

THE METAL RICE BOWL

In college, it was easy to pinpoint the rich by the cars they drove and the clothes they wore. The affluent also knew how to navigate the hidden job market through their influential network. For the rest of us, we had to compete against the masses in the advertised job market. I was likely competing with more qualified candidates because I was consistently rejected without even an interview. It was not surprising since my resume only consisted of part-time jobs throughout high school, and to land an engineering internship, I knew that I had to create my own connections.

After countless rejections, I finally landed my first internship at an engineering firm in the summer after my freshman year. My roommate, Jack, had secured the interview for me because his dad was a senior executive at the company. During the interview, I exaggerated my relationship with Jack's dad even though I had never met him. I talked up fishing stories as if we were old acquaintances. At the end of the interview, I was hired instantly as an office engineering technician.

The adrenaline rush from my first paid college internship kept me up all night like I had a rock and roll band playing in my head. With indecipherable lyrics that didn't have much meaning, I finally gave in to the deafening noise and got out of bed to prepare for my first day on the job. I looked out the window—the golden disc seemed to be rising and rising, and the birds were singing to its shine and celebrating my first paid college internship. I had never noticed the exquisiteness of the rising sun, but that morning, I was mesmerized by its reddening beauty and wanted to stop time to capture that beautiful moment of a new beginning. I washed up, hummed a few Elvis tunes, and put on a white dress shirt paired with a red power tie that blended perfectly with my only navy-blue suit. The mirror reflected a poised and self-assured young man ready to take on the world.

I arrived at the office early and was greeted by the receptionist who informed me that Rose, the executive assistant to the president, would be my boss. After some small talk, Rose gave me my first assignment—to wash all the coffee mugs and dishes in the sink from the day before and then deliver five sets of blueprints to clients whose offices were spread throughout Los Angeles. Although surprised at the non-engineering assignment, I didn't want to question her and quietly proceeded to the kitchen, removed my jacket and tie, and put on an apron to ensure that the liquid soap did not splash on my immaculate white shirt. After driving all over town delivering building schematics, I barely made it back to the office before closing time. I went to my boss's office to say goodbye, and she told me nonchalantly, "Just wear your tees and jeans for the rest of the summer. This is a delivery job." My heart sank with disappointment when I realized that I was not going to be an engineering intern.

Two weeks into the job, I reached out to the firm's chief engineer and asked for an opportunity to shadow him and learn about engineering. He looked at me and said, "Does your boss know that you are here to see me?" I pleaded to him, "No. And she doesn't have to know." The next day, I was transferred to the drafting room, and I became an engineering technician with my own desk and drafting table. I ran to the bathroom and screamed with excitement while pumping both fists in the air over and over like Rocky Balboa. That was the first time I didn't wait for good things to happen to me. I was not frozen in fear. I took control and didn't wait for life to happen to me.

With experience in a reputable engineering firm under my belt, I found a job pretty quickly as a logistical specialist for the Los Angeles County Sanitation Department the following summer. On the first day, I found out that the job involved opening cast iron utility hole covers and testing the air quality before the engineers could safely go underground to inspect, test, and clean the cast iron sewer lines. In addition, every Friday between 10 p.m. and 6 a.m., I would test and record air quality readings from these large, galvanized water tanks located in an isolated industrial area by myself. During the first day of training, I opened my first maintenance hole cover with a giant crowbar called a manhole key that weighed at least a ton. As soon as the metal lid was lifted, these massive, scavenging cockroaches began scattering and hurling themselves toward corners, looking for refuge in cracks and crevices. Some tumbled and fell to the bottom of the chamber floor, while others disappeared into the fissures of the concrete wall.

Even though I grew up with cockroaches in Hong Kong, the pungent smell of acid and mold made me gag, and I teared up immediately. My supervisor looked at me disparagingly and said, "You will get used to this." She then put on her wet suit and mask and climbed down the concrete chamber just large enough to fit one person. For the next three days, the same scene repeated itself like the movie *Groundhog Day*, and each time it felt like the worst job I ever had. Then came Friday, and I had to go test the air quality in water tanks located in some secluded, pitch-black industrial location. My work area was an open ledge mounted on the edge of the water tank. There were no visible bathrooms, and my job was to climb up the metal ladder, throw in the measuring instrument, record the readings, and repeat the process every hour. I wished they had a statement on the application that read, "Due to extreme darkness, the applicant must not have nyctophobia." I would not have applied since my fear of the dark started in childhood and never entirely left me. The place was eerily quiet, and I began to irrationally torment myself, "What if I got murdered and got tossed into one of the tanks? Would anyone even notice that I went missing other than my family?" The more my mind wandered, the more scared I became. It was one of the longest nights of my life. The following Monday, I went and talked to the head of engineering and told them about my experience working in an engineering firm the summer before, and he immediately transferred me to the engineering department in an air-conditioned office. I learned that having the courage to ask was something we all have control over.

Next summer, I worked three times a week as a teaching assistant at an elementary school where students were predominantly from Vietnamese families that had immigrated to America to seek better lives for their children. I saw myself in them, but I didn't know how to mentor them or point them in the right direction. I told them to study hard and get into the best university they possibly could. They just laughed in my face and told me that college is not for people like them. I felt a sadness come over me. They had given up hope like I had.

To supplement my income, I also taught math to burly construction men and women at the Mexican American Opportunity Foundation. I became good friends with my students, and they threw me a big party with plenty of alcohol on my last day and were shocked at the amount of liquor my skinny body could hold. We drank into the wee hours, shared stories, and truly enjoyed our friendships.

Through each job, I learned to connect with people and ask for opportunities to increase unexpected outcomes. Toward the end of my senior year and for the first time in America, I started thinking seriously about my future. I thought about what I loved as a kid outside of basketball, pastimes that I really enjoyed doing, or events that had shaped my life. Immediately I ruled out basketball because I knew I didn't have the physicality to play at a professional level. I also eliminated politics since it did not meet the return on my time from a monetary standpoint. I enjoyed meeting new people, striking up conversations with strangers effortlessly, and bringing people together at parties, but in the end, I had chosen engineering as a career because math was easier for me than grammar. Ultimately, the decision was about not being poor anymore, and engineering was a respected profession that paid handsomely.

This is when prosperity began, or so I thought.

UCLA gave me a pedigree, and I was ready to make a mark in the world. I must have sent out at least 100 resumes and cold-called twice as many. Most of my friends already had at least one job offer from a top-tiered aerospace company, and some even received multiple offers. With a glamorous resume that flaunted eclectic internships delivering blueprints for a small engineering firm, opening utility covers, testing the air quality for a government sanitation department, and teaching math at a nonprofit organization, I was not very competitive against my peers. With zero job offers and mounting student loans staring me down, my decision was going to be based on who could pay me the most money.

Finally, after a long, frantic job search, I received two job offers. One was from California Institute of Technology as a research assistant for a professor and another from a family-owned manufacturing company that designed and built microprocessor controllers. I chose the latter just because it paid more. The company employed four people: the owner/president, his secretary, a software engineer, and a hardware engineer. The entire building consisted of four offices and a room equipped with oscilloscopes, similar to the labs in some of my college courses. My responsibility as the fifth employee was to help debug a program that the software engineer had written.

On my first day of work, I arrived at the office in the early dawn with a bright outlook for my future. My enthusiasm was only surpassed by watching a live Bee Gees concert the night before. After meeting with the software engineer, I was given a thick stack of computer printouts and tasked with finding the errors in them. I don't quite remember what the programming language was, but I had no idea what I was looking for exactly. That night, I went to Borders Bookstore and bought a bunch of programming books and began training myself at night. I found three errors in the first twenty pages of codes, with at least 2,000 more pages left to go. It was an arduous task, but somehow, I completed my first assignment, although not within the timeframe I was given.

I was ecstatic when I received my first paycheck. I spent half of my paycheck and sent the other half to Ah Ngyin, but the check to her was never cashed. I was not sure whether she did not receive it, or she didn't know who it was from since my Chinese writing at this time was atrocious. Ah Ngyin passed away in 1991 at ninety-five years old. I regretted not having visited her in Hong Kong like my brothers did. She will always have a special place in my heart.

In my second month, I was reassigned to work with the hardware engineer in the test lab, which I hated in college. I thought I was done with oscilloscopes, but there I was again, staring at the apparatus with much disdain. I was asked to begin testing all these prototype machines, and I had no idea where to start.

Three months later, I walked into the office and immediately felt the stiff air taking away some of the oxygen in the room. The secretary looked at me, nodded, and without our habitual pleasantries, continued working. An hour later, she knocked on my door and told me the president wanted to see me. My heart started palpitating on the long walk to the president's office. In my mind, I was getting either a promotion or a bonus for my hard work. However, to my chagrin, he asked me to sit down and without any polite greetings, stoically said, "You are a nice kid, but things aren't working out. We will pay you through the end of the day." That was it. He then asked me to close the door on my way out. In disbelief, I staggered back to my office as if a truck had hit me, and with tears welling up in my eyes, began packing up all the programming books that I was never reimbursed for buying. On the drive home, I cried uncontrollably and wished that I had studied harder in college and made friends with those oscilloscopes.

Let's backtrack. I attended UCLA for my undergraduate degree and studied electrical engineering during my four years. I would love to say I put in eight hours a day, seven days a week mastering the theory of electronics engineering—circuits, design, hardware, electromagnetics, diodes, transistors—but I regret that was not the case. When I should have been learning integrated circuit design, I was practicing my three-point shot. When I should have been studying the fundamentals of semiconductors, I was working on my left-handed layup. When I should have been applying electromagnetic field theory to solve real-world problems, I was taking step-back jump shots. It is safe to say I spent a lot more time playing basketball than studying. I wished I had played less basketball, drank less beer, and devoted myself more to the books.

In the '80s, electrical engineering was a burgeoning and competitive field, similar to the state of computer science today. My friends were getting hired as engineers at all sorts of companies in both the private and public sectors, and I believed that graduating with an electrical engineering degree would set me on a safe path toward a stable career. My ultimate goal was to get a job, become self-sufficient, and help my family. I may not have realized it at the time, but I lacked any attachment to electronics engineering as a specialization and engineering as a discipline. I think to truly maximize your potential in something, regardless of what it is, you have to really love what you do. My decision to pursue engineering was largely influenced by knowing that graduating with that major would allow me to acquire a job quickly and easily, which to my family meant career and life stability.

My self-pitying thoughts were interrupted by a gentle knock on my door, and the hardware engineer came in, shook my hand, and wished me luck. That was the end of my first job. It lasted three months. One season or the length of time it took my intramural basketball team to win it all. A UCLA degree opened a few doors from prospective employers, but ultimately, I was exposed for my incompetence to carry out an entry-level engineering job. I was devastated at being fired but even more worried for my future. I didn't want the sun to rise the next day.

But there is always a silver lining amid the chaos. Being unemployed and incapable of paying rent, I moved back in with my parents and enrolled in the Master of Electrical Engineering program at California State University in Los Angeles, with a specialization in Systems Engineering. I needed to explain the employment gap by making it look like I had quit my first job to get an advanced degree. But graduate school was difficult, and I struggled with some of the concepts, and worse, with motivation. Luckily, I met a friend who breezed through all our classes together, and he offered to help me with my homework. With a lifebuoy in place, I would play basketball during the day, rush to meet my friend before class to do homework, check the job board, and attend classes at night.

During a routine morning, I saw on the job board that the Department of Water and Power (DWP) was looking to hire an electrical engineer with an MS degree as a desirable qualification. I applied even though I was barely into the program, went through a series of interviews, and succeeded. I was offered a government job in the largest public utility company in the nation, and the pay was great! I proved to myself that I was intelligent, made good impressions, and could sell myself. I can't say I have a passion for engineering, but my confidence grew with the prosperous outcome.

The family, with an emphasis on my parents, was ecstatic that I had gotten a job as an engineer for the government. For them, this job was not only a new conversation piece among their neighbors and friends—something like hitting the Chinatown jackpot—but more importantly, it was reassurance that the decision to move to America and the sacrifices they had made were worth it. Like most Asian immigrants, my parents valued stability over risk. They did not care what type of engineer I was; they were simply satisfied knowing that if I performed my work satisfactorily and stayed with the company long enough, I would be promoted and have a stable life for myself. In Asian countries, getting a civil service job required a series of tests that were considered difficult, like a bar exam. Civil servants were respected for their authority, and a government job was considered prestigious.

My parents felt that I had made it, meaning I could now live independently, find a wife, settle down, and have kids. In their eyes, I had achieved a successful career, a good salary, and homeownership would just be right around the corner, all in less than two years out of college. My life was already beyond their hope for me. I had found my Gold Mountain! A government job for life. Isn't that what the American dream is all about?

The DWP is the nation's largest municipal utility and has arguably the most powerful union on earth in the sense that every past and current politician who proclaimed they could reform its management had failed 100 percent of the time. I spent my first two years designing a new state-of-the art control system for the water department. Our goal was to update the old analog systems with digital technology which increased the efficiency, speed, and reliability of the entire water distribution network. I know, fascinating stuff.

My boss was a guy named Green, a snarky man who was not intimidated by anyone, not even his bosses but to everyone's surprise, we hit it off right from the get-go. He would come to my house to pick me up for business trips, and on a few occasions, he even stayed for dinner at my parents' house before we headed out to the airport. He would sit at the dinner table just to placate my parents, but since he wasn't a fan of authentic Chinese food, we would always end up at McDonald's for a Big Mac before taking our seats on the plane.

On our trip to Boston to get trained for the new computer system, I was sick the entire six-hour plane ride, and Green helped check me into the hotel, brought dinner to my hotel room, and made sure I was fine before he left. I felt so appreciative but ashamed that I never outgrew my motion sickness. Eventually, I came down with the flu and ended up spending a week in my hotel room to recover.

While my projects were far from strenuous, and my work-life balance was heavily skewed in the direction of life, the work itself was not very fulfilling. As kind as the job was to me, designing circuit systems was not the most exciting task, nor one that I could see myself continuing long-term. Bored out of my mind, I decided to transfer to the power side of the company, fixing antiquated relay systems to control the flow of electricity more efficiently. I know, that sounds like a lot of jargon, but essentially, my job was to design the circuits that directed electricity from the generating stations to, say, individual houses or buildings. If I did my job correctly, when you turned on a light switch, the distributive networks should have directed electricity to that specific light fixture. I stayed loyal to the business unit I was in, hoping to position myself for an eventual promotion.

Since Civil Service rules were enacted to prevent nepotism and guarantee fairness, the bureaucratic inertia made advancements very difficult. Promotions were 50/50, meaning it was based 50 percent on a written test, which was all technical, and 50 percent on an interview, and the final score was calculated based on the average two scores. To climb the corporate ladder, I knew I needed more education to ultimately compete for C-suite positions, and with that goal in mind, I continued and completed a Master's in Systems Engineering degree in two years.

Around my eighth year at DWP, I applied for an entry-level management role. I finished the final interview in half an hour and felt pretty confident about my performance. At the time, I was very good friends with the department's secretary, who oversaw the process of entering all the final applicants' scores into a spreadsheet for the hiring manager to mull over. The secretary told me, in confidence of course, that I had finished with an overall score of 98. I was over the moon—reassured that the master's degree was worth the time and that management was indeed my calling. Knowing the high score from the interview, I was certain the position was mine, and a bit arrogantly, I even went car shopping that night.

The following week, I received a call from my boss to come to his office, which was unusual because he usually came straight to my office to talk to me. After exchanging informal chats, he delivered the discouraging news straight to the gut, "Sorry, Ed, you did extremely well, but unfortunately, one question separated the first and second spots, and we are required to hire the candidate with the highest overall score. So, we're going to give the job to Mr. Giovani." Ouch! He tried to soften the blow by positively explaining that the position would be mine when Giovani retires in the next couple years. Great, I was an afterthought.

There had to be some unaccounted factors that catapulted Mr. Giovani in front of me, and I was dumbfounded. The next day, I followed up with my boss to ask how I could have done better and was told that I outperformed everyone with the highest score, but that he wanted Giovani to leave with a higher pension upon retirement. I was appalled at the unspoken "seniority over merit" rule. I had lost the job to someone who had been there for thirty-five years, just waiting to retire for the last two. The implicit rule meant that for me to get promoted, I would have had to wait two more years, and I was unwilling to do that. For the duration of that month, my motivation for the job was steadily declining.

After pouting for about a week, I went over my boss's head directly to the division's senior executive and asked for a transfer. Without any pep talk or trying to persuade me to stay, he told me that project management was an area that provided an opportunity to develop leadership skills far beyond my current engineering role, and that if I was interested, he would help secure an interview for me in this new division. I knew that my existing engineering position would not prepare me for vertical growth within the company and told him I was extremely interested in this new role.

Three days later, I met with Hank, the senior executive in the project management division, to discuss the new opportunity, and a week later, I started a new job as an assistant project manager in charge of a team that was responsible for bringing in new sources of electricity from out-of-state partners. Thankfully, as a project manager, I no longer had to perform tedious calculations or analyses. Instead, my new role was scheduling, budgeting, and solving unforeseen problems that the team would inevitably face in a complex project. The new position was my first exposure to managing people rather than processes, forcing a fundamental shift in how I approached work, set goals, and accomplished tasks.

Different individuals require different forms of motivation; some engineers respond to a time crunch, others need more verbal prodding. Over time, I learned that my role was more of a hybrid facilitator-coach: develop a roadmap for the project, select the human capital necessary to complete it, and ensure each team member did their job well. Strategically, I had to understand the skills and motivation of each member, and collectively, maximize the strengths and minimize weaknesses of the team. To stay on track, I had to rally the team toward a shared vision, demonstrate both optimism and self-confidence to overcome setbacks, and show resilience when things went wrong. To say I fell in love with the role was probably an understatement, and over the next three years, I had developed a passion for management. Whether it was diffusing a misunderstanding, finding a remedy to an internal problem, or guiding my team toward the finish line, a fire had been lit under me.

I enjoyed the job and relished meeting new people. The project management experience taught me that it was not the smartest or best engineers who ran the show, but the best communicators. I remembered stammering and sweating profusely through a quarterly update in front of many utility executives, and to calm my nerves down, I just read the remaining report verbatim, not making eye contact with anyone. It was an epic failure. I knew I had to overcome my fear of public speaking if I wanted to be a manager someday. All the top executives had a business degree and were articulate, eloquent speakers.

Eventually, I was promoted to the position of manager overseeing one of the largest inter-agency projects, which required me to move to Las Vegas. The move also coincided with the time that Cathy and I were struggling with infertility, but we both felt that the job would give us a break from the stress of trying to conceive after years of unsuccessful attempts.

After a successful stint in Las Vegas, I moved back to Los Angeles to perform administrative work that did not require me to be on site. The utility industry was in the process of deregulating, and for the first time in its nearly century-old monopoly existence, DWP faced competition and had to protect its customer base. In response, DWP reorganized the company and created a Marketing Business Unit to compete in a free marketplace. The reorganization resulted in four directors, and each got to pick four senior managers to oversee specific business sectors. The process to select the sixteen senior managers took over three months, and it was during these precarious times that I thrived. A new type of engineer had to be created, one who could succinctly explain technical concepts, justify its rates, and connect with customers. It was a chance for engineers to move into the business world with the promise of fast-tracked promotions if things worked out. The position was perceived as a career-making move and coveted by many.

The turning point for my dull engineering career came when I received the phone call from Dale, one of the directors. He coyly asked, "Are you ready to get to work?" Without hesitation, I said emphatically, "Yes!" I was one of a handful of engineers selected to lead the company into the uncharted waters of a deregulated industry. I was excited beyond belief with the promotion. I had finally made it. I was on top of the world.

Dale was a hulking presence at 6'4", had immaculate gray hair, and wore well-pressed Italian suits. He spoke in a modulated voice, was eloquently articulate, and carried an air of gravitas that commanded respect. Prior to meeting Dale, my early management style was shaped from the lessons learned playing basketball. I learned that players just wanted a fair chance to compete, and the most successful coaches were fair, sold players on a vision, leveraged players' strengths, and helped each player grow individually. After I started my career, I learned leadership and management practices from the autobiographies of successful business CEOs like Steve Jobs, Warren Buffet, and Jack Welch.

While basketball lessons and books set the foundations of my management philosophy, Dale was the first mentor who took an interest in me, but more importantly, he believed in me more than I believed in myself. He gave me the opportunity of a lifetime and a chance at developing my real-world leadership skills. Together, we were a formidable team and signed up three of the largest commercial users from a competitor. The new agreements wreaked havoc across the industry and prompted the threat of lawsuits from our private-sector rivals. To immerse myself on the business side, I began to pursue a formal MBA program to learn more about strategy, marketing, finance, and people management. However, the short-lived deregulation experiment resulted in rolling blackouts, skyrocketing utility rates, and alleged trading fraud, and soon after, the marketing unit also imploded. All the senior marketing managers were demoted back to their former positions and as I reverted back to engineering, I also became dissatisfied with my work. The thought of continuing to work in a civil service system that valued seniority over talent just didn't resonate with me anymore, and I quickly realized that even if I had graduated with an MBA, I would still have to go through the antiquated government system and wait for my turn in the civil service succession queue for another ten years to be promoted.

The desires of my heart and mind began to diverge. Although my mind was content with the salary, my heart was beating to a different drum, crying out for oxygen in a stifling system. Of the nine hours I spent at work, eight of them were spent counting the minutes and seconds before I was off. For the first time in my life, I began questioning the purpose of work, and believed that I was destined for greater impact. The only way I imagined myself getting out of bed every morning was going to work for a company whose passion was aligned with mine.

The more people I met from other industries, the more I began to understand my true strengths: I connected with people easily and was great at sensing the unarticulated needs of others. After two years of business simulations, case studies, and experiential projects, I was eager to test my newfound theoretical management skills in an industry that genuinely valued great people, managers, and innovators. I was ready to take a risk at trading in stability for a merit-based system of rewards.

With lingering thoughts about my purpose in life and the impact of my work, I knew in my gut that I wanted to work for a company that was going to change the world. I began planning my exit and began interviewing with private sector companies. When I relayed the news to my parents, they were distraught and could not understand why I was getting antsy. I still remember my dad lecturing me in Chinese, "How can you leave a metal rice bowl on the table for someone else to take!?" My mom pleaded with me, "You are living the American dream! You have a stable job with a bright future. Why throw it all away!"

My parents still had a very traditional heritage and mindset, and for them, working at DWP was the pinnacle of career success: the job was generally not high stress, offered medical benefits, and most importantly, it came with a pension that grew based on years of service—the more years you worked, the higher your pension became. In my parents' eyes, leaving DWP was equivalent to abandoning a life of guaranteed stability, the dream they made countless sacrifices for so that we could live a more leisurely life than they did.

I understood their point of view. In the Chinese culture, a low-risk career path defined by stability and high pay was greatly encouraged. They made the sacrifice so we could live a good life, which I had achieved, and yet, I was now prepared to throw it all away to work in private industry where stability was not guaranteed—to them, this was illogical. From their perspectives, DWP was a "metal rice bowl" career, a metaphor for a life of stable employment and decent wages. Traditionally, the bowls Chinese used were made of cheap ceramic, easily broken if dropped, but also inexpensive enough to replace. In contrast, a metal bowl was made out of iron or steel and was far more expensive. When a metal bowl is dropped, it does not break; it may make a loud noise and be slightly dented, but it can still be used over and over.

To placate them, I found a director-level managerial job at a smaller utility company doing exactly what I did at DWP but with higher pay. Coincidentally, DWP was experiencing financial trouble and the senior leadership wanted to entice people to retire early or leave the company to reduce payroll. As soon as the terms of the retirement package were announced, I made the first available appointment with Human Resources, and many pen scribbles later, I sealed my fate and gracefully left DWP. Even though I had already landed firmly with a smaller utility company, my parents were still a bit disappointed in me, not because they did not believe in my capabilities, but because I had their American dream in the palm of my hand and instead of grasping it tightly, I let it go. They didn't feel that the smaller company had the same prestige and opportunity as a large behemoth like DWP. Deep in my heart, I knew that the new job was just moving from one government system to another. Once again, I had chosen stability over risk. I will forever be grateful for the opportunities that DWP gave me early on in my career, and if not for that project management experience, I would not have discovered my love for people management.

On the first day of the new job, the CEO asked me why I didn't apply for the higher executive position, which he thought fit me perfectly. I told him I did but that their civil service system disqualified me from the list due to a lack of qualified years of experience. I was looking forward to a fresh start, but to my surprise, the higher position went to Dale, my former boss at DWP, which meant he would be my direct administrator once again. After almost a year, it became abundantly clear that I would be doing the same thing for the same boss except with a different company. I felt suffocated and my growth stunted. With dual masters in engineering and business under my belt, I was unwilling to get stranded in the molasses structure of civil service again. Even though it was hard to leave a steady paycheck and go into the unknown, I knew that I would have to take the chance and start a career with a company whose product I was passionate about supporting.

After a month of applying to a few companies whose products I connected with, I was hired as the Director of Operations at the *Los Angeles Times*, reporting to a well-respected industry veteran with a stellar reputation. The transition from engineering to business was exciting and intimidating at the same time. Finally, I chose risk over stability and heart instead of logic. All my life, I made decisions based on avoiding pain and living a comfortable life. Now I was ready to break the rules and strive for innovation that the private sector is so famous for leading.

10

THE EXECUTIVE

I felt like I had it all: a beautiful wife, a burgeoning family, and a new calling. All my life, I valued job stability above all else, and this was my opportunity to prove to myself that my abilities could translate into the private sector. I was beyond thankful for the last fourteen years at DWP, and quite frankly, spoiled to have been able to raise a family under very steady conditions. But I was excited to kick off my new journey with the incredible and talented storytellers who helped people understand how the world works every day.

The *Times* was truly an incredible company with exceptional journalists who were able to break down complicated ideas and events through human stories that evoked compassion and empathy in all of us. The product gave voices to underserved communities, shed light on the disadvantaged, held the government accountable, and provided access to entertainment pre-Google days. The more intimate I became with the product that I not only admired but consumed daily, the more I appreciated the passion of the people behind its mission. It was truly a dream job to be part of producing something that really made a difference in people's lives.

The first week, I concentrated on understanding the entire content creation, printing, and delivery process, a 24/7 operation the *Times* proudly called the Daily Miracle. I was required to go on a ride-along program designed to get new hires familiarized with the entire operation, but from the stop-and-go motion, I got nauseous (again). However, after three months, I felt that my role resembled more of an engineering job, only now it was with a different company, and I didn't give up my stable government job to essentially do the same work. I felt capable of doing more, wanted to do more, and was hungry to do more. I wanted the opportunity to live to my full potential and have a more impactful life. Slowly, regret started creeping in, and I was ready to leave the *Times* to pursue a more meaningful career than just looking for ways to cut costs in the supply chain.

During dinner that evening, I told Cathy that I was dissatisfied with my career trajectory and felt confined in my cocoon of mediocrity. She immediately understood what I was feeling, acknowledged my frustration, and encouraged me to go find my calling. She had gone through similar transitions from working as a grant writer for a nonprofit organization to finally finding her calling as an educator.

The phone rang, and we both ignored it. We made it a point not to pick up the phone during dinner unless it was an emergency. When the answering machine kicked in, it was from the SVP of the company. I ran to pick up the phone while he was leaving a long voicemail and greeted him just in time. In a very calm voice, he informed me that the chairman said he was impressed with my thoughtful questions during a company-wide meeting, and that if I had the courage to ask questions on everyone's minds, he wanted to take a chance on me. In disbelief, I told Cathy what had just happened, and we both burst into happy tears and ended up staying up the rest of the night until the birds started chirping in the background as if they were wishing me good luck. The final step was to meet with Matt, the chairman of *Times Mirror*, to assess my abilities and how well I might fit into his company's culture.

I was scheduled to see Matt at 9 a.m., and I checked in promptly at 8:30 a.m. I was nervous and rehearsing in my mind what I was going to say to him. My stomach was in knots, and I remember telling myself repeatedly, "This is the opportunity I have been waiting for, and I have to seize the moment. This is my shot. I can't fail." As I was mentally practicing my pitch, I was interrupted by Matt's executive secretary, and in a soothing voice she said, "Matt will see you now."

I walked into Matt's 2,000-square-foot penthouse office which had an unobstructed view of the uneven zigzag skyline of downtown LA. His desk was immaculately organized with pictures of his family, and a few of Jack Welch's books caught my eyes. While trying to get a closer read of the titles, a man with wire-rimmed glasses and perfectly groomed hair came in from another door that was not visible from the outside. He looked more like a professor than a CEO, and with a fatherly smile, he motioned for me to sit on the couch across from him.

He greeted me cordially and said, "Make yourself comfortable. And please just call me Matt." After the table talk, he asked me earnestly, "How do you feel about being a VP of the executive team?" I responded enthusiastically, "It is an opportunity that I won't squander." He then asked, "Why do you think we can grow the *Times* by one million in circulation?" I responded confidently, "I know that the industry veterans and even our own senior executives don't believe that it is a realistic goal, but I believe lofty goals breed innovation. I believe it is possible with the right leadership. We have been thinking about the *Times* from a newspaper perspective. We need to pivot and think of the *Times* as one of the biggest brand products in the world. Give me two years to make it happen." He looked at me, nodded, and said, "Congratulations, Ed, and welcome to the executive team." That was it. Two questions that changed the trajectory of my life. I was now a bona fide Fortune 500 executive, a status shared by an elite segment of the population. Every aspect of my life was about to change. I felt like my entire career path had culminated with this dream job, but little did I know that when I started labeling this promotion as a "dream job," I was limiting my growth and setting myself up for failure.

The news that the most coveted job at the *Times* went to an outsider with no newspaper experience reverberated across the company. The executive I would be replacing was a well-respected industry expert and regarded as indispensable. The rumor was that he openly challenged the chairman's lofty goal to exponentially grow circulation by one million units, which was an impossible task by industry standards. The newsroom was also flabbergasted and publicly denounced such impossible demands. But I truly believed that it could be done. It took time, but just like I did in basketball, I knew that if people felt safe, heard, and valued, they would perform exceptionally.

Slowly, the team was coming together, but now we had to find a way to work with our editorial partners. Even though the product's content was unquestionably outstanding and consistently recognized as one of the top three newspapers in the country, the newsroom was, to a certain degree, hubristic over the superiority of the paper's content. But together, we worked across silos to break down the business-editorial divide. Eventually, the newsroom relented, and a pilot program bundling the *Times* with the largest circulating Spanish paper in Los Angeles was initiated, followed by a similar agreement with the largest Chinese newspaper six months later. Immediately, the

Times had grown by more than 300,000 units, and the addition catapulted the paper to become the highest circulated metropolitan daily newspaper in the country. For our herculean efforts, I was given the innovation award of the year. The best part was that the entire team was rewarded with hefty stock options.

I loved that we could use our imaginations to create new possibilities and business models that got us closer to a million. From a leadership perspective, I learned that leaders must have values, and to be effective, those values had to be aligned with the organization's values without moral conflict. Equally important, behaviors must always reflect values because employees must believe in their leader's actions for a culture to thrive. It is good to be exceptional in business, but it is better to be great at managing people and relationships. As much as we want to think that we can do it alone, all significant accomplishments come from working together as teams. The best ideas don't mean a thing if you can't inspire people toward a common goal. Perhaps one day I will become a leadership expert, maybe even get a doctorate in leadership.

I was truly living the American dream and, with the hefty salary plus all the stock options, I could have bought any car I wanted to, but instead, I continued to park my ten-year-new Nissan Pathfinder on the executive level that resembled a luxury car lot of Lexus, Porsche, Corvette, BMW, and Mercedes. Even though the SUV had no electric windows, I continued to drive it as a reminder to stay authentic and true to my humble beginnings, with the additional perk of not worrying about getting dings from other cars. One morning Matt saw me get out of my SUV and jokingly said, "Ed, do I not pay you enough?" I smiled and said, "Not for the work I am doing." He laughed and said, "Keep up the good work." However, after straining my lower back reaching over to the passenger door to manually pull up the lock and let someone in, I decided to install an aftermarket electric lock system for the doors. But the arduous commute between La Mirada and Los Angeles eventually took its toll on the SUV, and after determining that the cost of repairs greatly outweighed the value of the car, Cathy finally convinced me to buy a new Acura MDX with fully loaded amenities, including electric windows and locks.

At this juncture, I was accumulating wealth beyond my wildest dream and, professionally, I was even on the masthead of the newspaper. However, to become a CEO, I knew I had to be a better communicator. All my life, I thought it was weak to cry in public. As an immigrant who crawled and fought my way up, I wanted to appear strong and composed so as not to perpetuate the weak stereotype. I hid my vulnerabilities and wanted people to see me only as confident, together, and in control. But when I saw Matt openly weep during a quarterly staff meeting, I was shocked! He got choked up when he spoke about the power of journalism and how the *Times* had changed more lives than any other products in the world. When Matt handed me the innovation award, he got misty-eyed and tenderly told me how proud he was of me, like a father would speak to his son. His raw public display of emotion that day changed my life; it was contrary to what I fought hard to hide and overcome all my life. If the head of a Fortune 300 company didn't care how he looked, why should someone much less accomplished care? Matt taught me not to be afraid of my weaknesses, and his actions gave me the courage to be my authentic self. From that day forward, I stopped following scripts and just spoke from my heart. I am eternally indebted to Matt for helping me embrace my vulnerability, but more importantly, using my upbringing as strength instead of weakness.

11

A TALE OF TWO COMPANIES

The phone rang during a routine dinner, and as always, we ignored it and continued talking. In a déjà vu moment, I heard my boss's voice leaving a message again. I ran to pick up the phone, and in a gloomy voice, he said, "We have been acquired by the Tribune Company. I just found out about it an hour ago and wanted you to hear it from me instead of finding out about it on the news." I thanked him and immediately turned on the TV, and the story was already being broadcast over several local channels. I wasn't sure what to think since I had never been through an acquisition before but was concerned about my future.

As publisher of the *Times*, Matt was a hopeless romantic who wanted to create a better world by injecting well-known business theories into the business. Most notably, he was influenced by Jack Welch's philosophy of "If you are not number one or number two in your market, get out," and reached deep down into every part of the organization to find innovation. In contrast, Tribune was a revered company known for its pragmatic money management practices. It was the classic "growth at all costs" versus "mining the balance sheet."

The stark deviation in leadership style was immediately felt down to the dress code. While Matt was the ultimate storyteller, a charismatic maestro who dressed in Armani suits—and I say that with the utmost respect and admiration for the man—the Tribune leadership team of CPAs arrived in plaid shirts, drab-colored slacks, and cowboy boots. But their laid-back demeanor did not reflect their decisive, breakneck pace. The new leadership team was handling discussions in secret and employees were given very little information. The following day, the head of HR under the former *Times* was kicked out of her office into a cubicle to help with the transition. Abruptly, our team dynamic and morale was gone.

The new leadership team then swiftly implemented a method similar to a casting process for the remaining senior management team to audition for a role with the new company. After the interview, if the executive was given a red envelope, he or she had until the end of the day to pack his or her belongings and leave. A green envelope meant that the executive was retained but at a lower position. The new leadership team kept their cards close to their vests, and everyone else just waited for their fate with the company.

The acquisition process took its toll on the retained employees and would have made a great case study on organized chaos.

I was not invited to a private meeting to receive a red or green envelope and was privately preparing my exit. Finally, after a couple of months, it was revealed that the reorganization created two new SVP positions, and the beneficiaries would be between Kelly, Sam, and me. In my mind, there was no debate as to who would get one of the two new executive positions. Sam was a former brand executive for a large consumer company and a proven expert in marketing. He exuded executive presence, an air of gravitas, and the confidence of someone who commanded respect. In our first meeting with the new leadership team, he handed out a high-level plan that spelled out how the company could grow moving forward. The plan wasn't over-the-top creative, it was actually pretty straightforward, but it was the right message. In my mind, we all had the same ideas, but he wasn't bashful, and his confidence sucked up all the air in the room. He delivered an intoxicating performance, a virtuoso in the room who had everyone eating out of the palm of his hand. He easily stood out among the three of us. A week later, the company announced Sam's new promotion. The question was who would get the last position. Was it going to be Kelly or me?

I was known as a charismatic leader with an innate ability to connect with people. Kelly was a long-time company loyalist with experience in many different parts of the newspaper business. We were friends, and when she reached out to me and asked if I would review her resume, I didn't hesitate and proceeded to recommend ways she could better communicate her qualifications. I expected one of the jobs to go to Sam but based on my flawed assessment, I didn't take Kelly seriously enough as a contender. In retrospect, I overestimated my own abilities and undervalued her experience. To strengthen my chances for the last coveted role, I reached out to Sam to ask for his support, and he enthusiastically told me that he would campaign for me to the new leadership team. But in a solemn tone, he also warned me, "I am not sure if the new company would want two Asian American males occupying the last two executive roles though."

The process took more than a month, and then it was announced that Kelly got the job, and I was offered a newly created, lower-level director position reporting directly to her. I didn't anticipate losing the job to Kelly, and my confidence was shaken. I had lost in the corporate reshuffling and felt that my window to becoming a CEO had just closed.

12

THE EXPIRED DREAM

Business leaders often use the phrase "change is inevitable" and a myriad of other change management theories to help leaders make smooth transitions. But when a merger happens, the blending of two cultures is an arduous task, especially if the cultures are distinctly different and the stakes and expectations are high. In the book *Who Moved My Cheese*, the brilliant author Spencer Johnson wrote a parable about the choices we have to respond to when unexpected changes occur. The lesson was about four characters who live in a maze, and they all love cheese, a metaphor for what we want in life. But when the cheese disappeared, Scurry and Sniff enthusiastically headed out to find new cheese, while Hem and Haw wasted their time and energy hoping the old cheese would return.

I had bought *Who Moved My Cheese* for my employees when I first became vice president to help them transition to the new company. Now the choice was staring me straight between the eyes. I wanted to be like Scurry and Sniff, who swiftly adapted, but instead I behaved more like Hem and Haw, unwilling to accept the inevitable change while waiting for the cheese to magically return. I became complacent as an executive for the *Times* before the Tribune acquisition. The job became my identity. It was my dream job, and I didn't want to wake up to a nightmare.

It was a seven-day roller coaster. Even though my past achievements were falling farther away with each passing minute, it was still hard to let go of the glorious past. My mind was like a pendulum swinging in supercharged mode. At one end, it was a chance at a new start with a title demotion but working for someone who I felt was not deserving of the job. At the other end, it was learning to be adaptable and trying to make the situation work. It was a gut-check decision.

I waffled five times over whether to quit or stay. I finally asked for a private meeting with the CEO to discuss my situation. During our meeting, he told me that years ago, he was also demoted in title to work on a special project, and when the project was completed, he was promoted to CEO of a smaller business unit owned by the parent company. He emphatically told me that he saw the same career path for me. I asked if I could report directly to him, and he said no, because he didn't have the time to mentor me but that his door would always be open if I ever needed his advice.

Before we parted ways, he said he needed a decision from me soon.

The next day, I went to the COO to assess his thoughts, and he invited me to his office. With a coffee in his hands, he greeted me cautiously and said, "Are you here to tell me the bad news or the good news?" I said incredulously, "What do you mean?" He led me to his computer and showed me all the emails between him, Kelly, and the CEO. They read, "Is he staying?" "He said yes but changed his mind." "He declined the job but changed his mind." "I think he is going to leave." "He wants to talk to you." I was embarrassed. I saw an irrational guy, and his indecisiveness and emotional instability was playing out before them. It was humiliating. I would not have wanted me! I told them I would give them a final decision in the morning.

Once again, I had trouble sleeping. My mind was playing ping-pong against the walls of my skull. One minute, my heart was screaming, "Don't take this shit," and then the next moment, my head was calmly telling me, "Change your perspective. Be like water." It was a tug-of-war with no clear winner. I instinctively knew that the company needed diversity on the senior executive team, and they already had one Asian in Sam. Finally, I convinced myself that it was just my ego talking. If they made a painstaking effort to keep me, I just have to change my attitude and not see it as a demotion but an opportunity to prove my worth. The next day, I accepted the new position.

I was at peace with the fact that I was no longer on the masthead. In reality, the path to the C-suite was no longer there for me. On the surface, it was a match made in heaven, marrying innovation and operations under one roof. Kelly was great at managing up and I was great at managing down except that there was no one reporting to me. We never argued during the entirety of our professional relationship. She was trying to survive the new management and was afraid to come across as weak and trusted that I would bring home the trophy to make us look good. The problem was we never talked about what that trophy looked like. Kelly never gave me any guidance on what I was supposed to do as the newly appointed director. After the formal organizational transition, I sold a couple of smaller papers for the company and got some praise from the CEO, which I guess kept me employed for another year.

Instinctively, I believed that multimedia was the heart and soul of the future, and we needed to look at other forms of distribution outside of the traditional print and TV platforms. I felt that we needed radio as a medium, and with the blessing of the CEO, began to explore the possibility of acquiring a couple of ethnic stations to complement the media portfolio that we already had in place. In between my research and analysis to identify acquisition targets, I divested a couple of smaller newspapers to cut debt to reduce the company's balance sheet.

In my heart, I no longer felt that we were working to make the company great. Instead, we were working to maximize the perceived valuation of the company. With shrinking the balance sheet being the top priority, I was asked by the CEO to put my business development activities on hold, and instead, set up special high-speed printers for our international offices located in five different countries. Because of the dissimilar time zones and the lack of prompt responses from our international offices, I couldn't report measurable status back to Kelly daily like she had wanted. Finally, our relationship turned sour when we disagreed on how we should operationalize the assignment.

As head of business development, I thought that at the minimum, I would be selling ads instead of counting them. However, she wanted something more discernible, something she could touch, measure, and control. Our vision of what my role should be began to diverge. I felt diminished in value.

Things turned very bad quickly. Overnight, she turned from a very supportive boss to a micromanager. The project was right up her project management wheelhouse, and it was something she felt she could tangibly control. She asked me to create a spreadsheet of the top five major newspapers and how many different sizes of advertisements were in each one. It was an easy enough task, so I asked my executive secretary to call all the papers Kelly had identified and purchase copies of each one. But the delivery process took about two weeks. I didn't think it was that big of a deal, but it was to Kelly. Suddenly, she wanted daily meetings with me to go over the status of this project. Furthermore, she wanted me to do this personally and not delegate it to my secretary. The excessive constraint was counterproductive to my value of autonomy, which relied on the currency of trust.

It was a painful two weeks. Her marching orders had hijacked my morale, minimized my brain capacity, and sucked all the oxygen out of me. I felt suffocated and devalued. However, I did not protest for fear of losing my dream job, which unbeknownst to me at the time, had already expired. While waiting for the newspapers to arrive, I became passive and just followed orders, hid in my office, and stopped taking risks. But as my frustration grew, my confidence shrank until I was a shell of my old self. I became a clock watcher, eager for the day to end. I began dreading Monday mornings and couldn't wait until Friday afternoons came around.

When the purchased newspapers finally came in, I measured each ad for size, grouped them into categories, and organized all the information into a spreadsheet. Thinking that I had completed the assignment, I created a PowerPoint deck describing how we could use the insights to develop a strategy for the type of advertisements the international offices could use in the new digital format. Hoping to turn around our strained relationship, I met with Kelly to discuss my findings and recommendations. Barely making eye contact with me, she thoughtlessly flipped through the PowerPoint, and with disdain and frustration, threw my slide deck into the trash can. I wasn't sure whether the sound was from my heart dropping to the ground or the PowerPoint deck hitting the bottom of the trash can, but suddenly, I could hear the blood splashing through my veins like waves crashing onto the shore. My heart was beating so loud that I was sure she could hear it too. In that one gesture, all the respect, trust, and relationship built over the last three years were destroyed. It was an attack on my self-esteem, and the gulf was too wide to ever be reconnected again.

Her face was flushed red, and her lips were quivering. But her facial expression only told half the story, her words made up the rest. She stared at me for thirty seconds, composed herself, and said, "This is useless information, and I can't believe it took you two weeks to put this together." She was visibly angry and exhausted at the energy she had to expend in micromanaging me. We had an intense staredown for what seemed like eternity, and for the entire duration to see who would blink first, the silence was deafening. We both recognized that we had reached an impasse in our professional relationship and friendship, that our disagreement was not simply over my work, it was just a bad fit.

Finally, when the tension had reached a crescendo, I looked at her and pleaded, "What were your expectations?" With visible fatigue on her face, she said with her raspy voice, "I need you to bring me back something concrete so that I can justify your existence." She furiously continued,

"People are talking behind your back. They told me that you are late every day, and you don't care about your job." I cut her off and retorted, "It is not people, it is one person, the finance director, and he told me he had talked to you." I continued sarcastically, "We are not in elementary school where kids tattle on each other." I threw up my arms to show my disbelief and continued, "I don't know what the company wants me to do. I don't know what you want me to do. I don't appreciate your micromanaging ways." I raised my voice and blurted out, "If you think someone can do a better job, we should part ways." As soon as those words came out of my mouth, I regretted it. Why couldn't I have just sat quietly and maybe tried to get better direction, mutually agreed to some goals, or get guidance from the CEO? But it was too late. She immediately said, "I accept your resignation." She picked up the phone, called HR, and within five minutes, a severance package was waiting for me to pick up.

Those fifteen minutes with Kelly changed my life. Our brewing issues were like termites eating at our relationship, and we were both miserable. It took a humiliating act for me to realize that I was a desperate man trying to hang on to the past. It wasn't so much what she said, but how she made me feel. Her condescending remarks were attacks on my parents' sacrifice as much as they were on my pride. The encounter was humbling but the experience did not cripple me. I needed to go where I would be celebrated and not simply tolerated.

The Tribune-Times Mirror merger was a corporate hangover and case study on cultural incompatibility. Tribune made a wrong bet, and their gamble uprooted the livelihood of many employees. Sometimes it takes bad circumstances for us to reflect on our shortcomings. The fear of losing my dream job had paralyzed me. I became too passive, stopped taking risks, and was focused more on preserving my job than looking for new opportunities. The *Times* experiment taught me to trust my own instincts and take risks in life. From that moment on, I vowed never to let anyone devalue me and compromise who I am ever again.

In 2005, the writing was on the wall as companies like Google were siphoning off ad revenues that once went to traditional publishing. The internet had become a utility, essentially, like water and power. The speed of getting news in real-time made the Tribune seem like pigeon carriers. As the company circled the drain, they attempted to rebrand its name to boost its image and bring the paper into the modern era. But amid growing mountains of debt and years of incessantly trying to cut costs to reach profitability, the Tribune finally imploded and declared bankruptcy.

While I had flirted with the idea of becoming a CEO for a Fortune 500 company, instead, I was now facing the prospect of standing in the unemployment line. My dream of becoming a CEO hit a pothole and was derailed like a train off its tracks. With my pride and self-esteem wounded, uncertainties staring at me, and an outdated resume in my hand, I didn't feel very optimistic about the future. Was it the end of the CEO journey for this sickly immigrant boy?

PART FIVE
THE ACCIDENTAL MAYOR

Let your values, not other people's expectations, define who you are and what you do.

The Thanksgiving Decision

1st Campaign Sign by Cathy

The Capeless Heroes

The Victory

The Celebration

Ready to Serve

The Accidental Mayor

13

MY TRAINING GROUND

There is always a silver lining in every dire situation. Without a work schedule to adhere to, I took on the responsibility of acting as Brandon's personal Uber driver—dropping him off and picking him up at school every day. Since I took on Brandon's school transportation responsibilities, Cathy was able to accelerate and complete her master's degree in education technology. When she graduated, I was ready to go back to work, but after a tumultuous two years under Tribune, I decided I wanted more work-life balance, more time to spend with family, and more time to watch Brandon grow up. I knew from my time at DWP that if I could work within the idiosyncrasies inherent in a government bureaucracy, the unhurried pace and slow decision-making process in the public sector could be an excellent place for a more stable life. Maybe my parents' philosophy of a nine-to-five, stress-free "metal rice bowl" career is superior to the cut-throat corporate grind.

I reached out to a couple of friends who worked for the county and was told by one of them that an executive position had just opened up in the county's Treasurer and Tax Collector office, a miniature department within a gigantic bureaucracy. I applied, interviewed, and was offered the job as a customer service executive to help the department run more efficiently. The job was a 60 percent pay cut from my last corporate job, but it promised a 9/80 schedule, meaning that I would have every other Friday off, essentially having twenty-four days off in addition to the two-week vacation plus holidays. With the growing paternal desire to spend more time with my son, I accepted the job.

Los Angeles County is easily the most populous county in the United States with more than ten million residents. County officials would always make the point that if Los Angeles County was a state, it would rank in the top ten in population among the fifty US states. From an economic standpoint, the county is greater than all but seven US states based on total Gross Domestic Product output.

The county's enormous size made the board of supervisors arguably the most powerful group of elected officials in the country. Under the county structure, the board had both legislative and executive power, which allowed them to have the ultimate control to set policy and make day-to-day decisions. However, the authority did not transfer to the CEO. Whereas in the private sector, a CEO would have free rein to hire or fire anyone at will, the county

CEO derived influence from having budget oversight of all the departments. The organization was very reactionary because crises always played out in public.

On Tuesdays, department heads who had an item on the board's agenda would be on standby in a conference room outside of the dais, in anticipation of being summoned to answer technical questions. But for the majority of the time, they sat quietly through mundane board meetings until the board wanted something, then instantly, the entire county came to a halt until the board got what they wanted. From time to time, I witnessed the board get yelled at by angry protesters, with some who even resorted to profanity. I remember thinking how much I admired the board for remaining calm and not responding to the name-calling during these raucous meetings. But no matter how harsh the criticism got, they still listened patiently and attentively. It was only later I learned that the Brown Act, or transparency law, prevented them from retaliating.

But most of the time, the eight-story Hall of Administration, home to the board, was a serene, quiet, and peaceful building until the board wanted something done or if something had made the headlines of the *Times*. Then, like a maestro in a symphony, a flick of the wrist would move all 100,000 employees synchronously toward the same direction to execute the board's motion to fix an actual or perceived debacle as reported by the *Times*. Although I was no longer employed by the *Times*, I continued to marvel at the mighty power of their ink. It is ironic that I once relished the role it played in society, and now I work for one of the largest bureaucracies in the nation.

Those experiences gave me a firsthand corporate box seat into how the government worked at its finest bureaucratic hours. While the *Times* proudly talked about the "daily miracle," a term they used to describe an uninterrupted service 24/7, I marveled at the complexity of the problems the board had to tackle daily. It is impossible to make ten million people happy, but when you throw in the demand and agendas of countless numbers of unions they had to negotiate with, it was truly a daily miracle how much the board accomplished. But one thing was for sure, I would never want to be a politician.

I was not shielded from the ultra-reactionary culture of the county. A short time into my venture back in government, I was invited by one of the boards district's senior deputies to attend one of their staff meetings to help facilitate a strategic planning session. The senior deputy said she heard me speak at a conference and thought that, given my business credentials, I had the talent to guide them in the right direction. A week later, I attended a full-day planning session and guided her team through the entire process. I didn't think it was that big of a deal and didn't bother to tell anyone. But when I casually recounted the activity at my department's senior staff meeting, the report immediately created a chain of emergency alerts as if I had committed espionage. I was interrogated as if I had broken some serious HR security policy: why I was summoned there, what was said, what time, and how it was received.

A few days later, several unwritten rules were established to deal with similar crises in the future. While my misconduct would have been applauded in the private sector, it was deemed a broken link in the chain of command that needed to be fixed. It was apparent that within the boundaries of this complex government behemoth, conformity and thinking inside the box behaviors often prevailed. I felt that the extreme reaction was unnecessary and knew that this job would be temporary until I went back into the private sector. However, instead of following extreme protocols, I simply declined all future meetings with any board offices.

After three months on the job, it was apparent to me that employees felt unmotivated because they were not appreciated by managers for what they had to endure every day. On a daily basis, front line staff were dealing with angry taxpayers who either wanted their property taxes reduced or late payment penalties waived. When these taxpayers did not get their way, they became combative and belligerent, and complained directly to the board. Then instantaneously, the grievances were escalated for priority responses, and the crisis management process began, even though the outcome rarely changed.

Sensing that it was an organizational cultural and not competency issue, I threw the antiquated and ineffective HR manual out the door and met each employee, gathered feedback, and based on my analysis, created an organizational structure that addressed pay inequity, process clarity, and service channel diversity. The process took three months, and the CEO swiftly approved the reorganization. I wasted no time implementing the changes.

The new environment had changed along with people's lives. I had promoted some employees, brought in technological innovation, and developed shared performance goals, and just like that, many of the efficiency metrics rocketed through the building. I had applied lessons that I had learned from my experience with Kelly: employees do not care what management says to them, they only care how managers make them feel. Employees desired human touch and appreciation for their work. I saw value in them when others didn't. I created a safe climate where everyone was heard, supported, and rewarded for their efforts. No, I didn't throw anyone's PowerPoint decks into the trash can either.

To express my deep appreciation for the team's hard work, I threw a Christmas party and took pictures with each employee in front of a nicely decorated tree. The same day, I developed the photographs and wrote a personal note to each one. A week later, as I was making my rounds in the office, I noticed that everyone had displayed a picture of us in their cubicles. I teared up instantly. The journey was worth it. Instead of rigid HR rules, the organization just needed a leader who would value their efforts, make them feel safe, and believe in their abilities more than they believed in themselves. Together, we created an environment where employees were more than just gatekeepers in a colossal bureaucracy, it was a place where they could thrive and prosper.

The one-year experiment turned into four years and, eventually, the quotidian routine began to wear on me. I also felt that we had reached optimal output, and each new idea became less efficient to implement. While the county was an excellent place to work without the demands of the private sector, I wanted more of a challenge and began putting feelers out to friends and executive search firms in the for-profit sector. I secretly fantasized that the county would create a consultant position that would combine the stability of the county and the creativity of the private sector. A quasi-consultant position that would allow me to go into each department, assess its structure and processes, provide rigorous analysis, and develop recommendations to make it more economical and efficient. Now that would be a dream job!

After a couple of interviews with a few small companies that did not result in any tangible offer, I came across a county job opening for an executive director position with a job description that resembled a private sector job but offered full benefits of the county. Essentially, a generalist with broad business knowledge to help them run more efficiently since specialists headed all thirty-six departments in their respective fields. The job promised independence from department executives and board offices, or in other words, an internal consultant job without any internal interference. I applied for the job and was hired the same day I had the interview.

The position turned into one of the best jobs I have ever held. The board offices kept their promises and never interfered with my work. They were very supportive of my findings and insights, and most of the recommendations have been either adopted or implemented, with a few stuck in civil service inertia. Most of the time, I was able to do my work without meddling from department heads, but occasionally, I would draw ire from a few executives because they didn't want to attract negative attention from board offices. One of them tried to discredit my findings before they went to the board offices, but since I had no desire to sit through long, arduous weekly Tuesday board meetings, I stood my ground knowing that my resistance would probably cost me a few promotional opportunities in the future.

Despite the constraints of antiquated civil service rules, I knew what I was getting into when I came back to work in government: I no longer had to contend with Wall Street expectations, stock price fluctuations, and the psychological turmoil of seeing people lose their jobs after an acquisition. Instead, what I learned was the quality-of-life issues that truly matter to people: the potholes, trimmed trees, and easy access to government. Perhaps my parents were right that the stability of a government job was the American dream, but I had to live through the private sector first, especially at the executive level.

The experiment at the *Times* was the experience of a lifetime but being back in government was a nice change of pace. Despite the self-affirmation, little did I know that all the bureaucracy that I despised so much like the Brown Act was something I had to deal with as a mayor.

14

SERENDIPITY

An unusual rainy southern California day became the starting point in my political journey. It was an atypical soggy day in La Mirada, and the deluge was flooding the streets. The warning lights came on, and my engine began to sputter and moan like a lawnmower. I drove into the first ingress that came up, which happened to be La Mirada City Hall. I proceeded into the parking lot and called AAA, who told me it would take at least two hours before they could get to me because so many calls were coming in through that day. I wasn't surprised—after all, southern Californians don't know how to drive on dampish roads. I called Cathy to let her know I would be waiting a while for AAA to tow my car home.

While waiting in my car, I looked up and saw a crowd of people going into City Hall, and curiously, I got out of my car to see what was going on since I had two hours to waste until AAA came. There was a big welcome sign that read "Coffee and Donut Mixer for Future Commissioners." Never one to pass up free donuts, I thought, "What the heck, these people don't know who I am."

It was the first time I had set foot in City Hall and to my surprise, there were no echoing concrete hallways, electronic checkpoints at entrances, or entry barriers to the building. As a first-generation immigrant, I stayed away from government buildings because they are intimidating to approach and even more confusing to navigate. But today, it was a far cry from the agitation and anxiety I had expected, the room had a heart, a rhythm, and a vibrant beat.

I went inside and the aroma of fresh donuts and coffee instantly transformed the room into a vibrant assembly atypical of government meetings. It was eerily comfortable to see all the smiling faces and people greeting each other inside a municipal building. After about a minute getting in line to sign in, it was obvious almost everyone knew each other. I put my name on a sign-in sheet and got a couple of sugar-frosted donuts and a cup of utilitarian coffee. I took a seat in the front row since no one else sat there and I would have more room to eat my donuts. Before I could get comfortable, the moderator pointed at me and said, "Would you like to go first, sir?" I was too embarrassed to tell them that I was here just for the free coffee and crullers while waiting for AAA, so I just got up and gave a bite-sized SWOT analysis (a technique for assessing the strengths, weaknesses, opportunities, and threats of a business) for the city. I remember saying something to the effect that outside of La Mirada and a few surrounding cities, no one even knew where La Mirada was, and to be considered a great community to live, people have got to be able to find you. From my perspective, the only association that people made with La Mirada is Derrick Williams, the phenom basketball player who made it to a D-1 college program (eventually into the NBA).

After two more donuts and sitting through another ten to fifteen more speeches, I tried to leave but didn't want to make it too blatant that I was there only for the free belly chokers. When the mixer ended, an older gentleman with immaculate white hair, glasses, and a well-tailored suit came up to me and introduced himself as Councilmember Steve DeRuse. He said, "Do you know what commission you want to serve on?" I said, "How many are there?" He patiently explained each one to me in detail, and at the end, he said, "Think about it over the weekend, talk it over with your family, and let me know which one you are interested in by next week." Another councilman came over and said he was impressed with my thought process and gave me his business card and asked me to call him.

After scarfing down four donuts, I lost my appetite for dinner. While fidgeting with my food and barely touching one of my favorite Filipino dishes, pancit, I told Cathy that a nice councilman asked me to serve on a city commission and another wanted me to call him. After talking it over with Cathy, we both felt that meeting once a month was not very demanding, and being on the Community Services Commission, we could find out more about city programs since we had attended a few in the past with our son Brandon. I called Councilman DeRuse first thing the following week, and I told him I would be interested in serving on the Community Services Commission.

During my time on the commission, I became really good friends with Jill, who graduated from Harvard with a master's degree in Public Policy. We created the inaugural strategic plan for the Community Services Commission, which was later used as a template to create the city's first comprehensive strategic plan. It was exciting, and without any intention of doing so, I playfully asked Jill what she thought about me running for City Council since there would be three openings coming up. Not sensing that I was joking around, she earnestly said, "Two incumbents are running, and the vacant seat created by an outgoing councilman already has a successor." Sensing my confusion, she went on to say, "I believe you would make a great councilman, but I already gave my endorsements to the two incumbents and the outgoing councilman's designated successor." I said incredulously, "What? The documents to formally qualify a candidate are not even due yet!" She calmly explained that prospective candidates sometimes have their endorsements lined up years in advance. Not to make her any more uncomfortable, I just dropped the subject.

I can't exactly describe the feeling that came over me that day. To the average person, learning that some political elections are predetermined years in advance is not breaking news. No one was breaking the law by building a succession plan before they exited office. I was not naive enough to believe this type of thing did not happen. But for me, this small piece of information just felt so wrong. My parents came to America with zero wealth, worked silently in menial jobs, and didn't have a voice in the system. I worked hard, I failed, and got back up time and time again. I learned how to survive in a world that I believe owed me nothing. To have lost more often than I have won, I felt that this preselection was another slap in the face to all the voiceless immigrants out there.

We always hosted family lunch and dinner on Thanksgiving Day for both sides of the family. After everyone had left, I asked Cathy and Brandon, "What do you think about me running for City Council?" Cathy asked, "Are you kidding? Do you know how to run a campaign?" To convince her of my earnestness, I went on a long-winded explanation, "No Asians have ever run for a city council seat in La Mirada. My purpose is not to make history, but the city now has almost 15 percent Asians, and if they all vote, I will have a real chance to win." She said, "I just never saw you as the political type, and how do you know the Asians will come out to vote for you?" I said in disbelief, "Because I am Asian!" To convince her further, I said, "You don't have to do anything. I will do all the work." She said, "Okay. But you did say I don't have to do any work, right?" I responded confidently, "One hundred percent!" I turned to Brandon and asked, "What do you think, Brandon?" Brandon just shrugged his shoulders and said, "Sure, Dad. Good luck."

I was an inexperienced outsider running for an elected office for the first time. That night, I consulted Google to learn how to run a campaign. All the articles I read from political pundits advised that the first thing to do is get endorsements from influential politicians and community leaders. I remembered being told that the political quilt of La Mirada was made up of some 200 leaders known as the La Mirada 200, those who are active in the community. Armed with this open secret, the following day, I reached out to a retired councilmember and invited him out to coffee to get some advice on how to run an effective campaign and also to get his endorsement. We met at IHOP, and he told me that La Mirada is a great city, and the majority of people are happy with the way the city is run, and based on historical voting patterns, residents would vote for the two incumbents, which meant the rest of the candidates would be vying for the one open seat vacated by an outgoing councilman. He said that while the city has seen a small growing share of Asian Americans, there has never been an Asian candidate before, and therefore he had no idea how residents would vote. He went on to say that although the city is small, it is still large in the sense that 99 percent of the people will have no idea who I am. He told me that to have a glimmer of hope, I desperately needed the endorsements of most, if not all, of the current and past councilmembers, commissioners, and people in leadership positions. Before he left, I asked for his endorsement, and he firmly said, "No." Over the next seven days, I managed to get hold of about fifteen current and past council members and commissioners, and I was met with either a firm "no" or "I already gave my endorsement to another candidate a year ago."

In less than twelve hours, my confidence began to wane from all the rejections. When you lose confidence, your mind begins to play tricks on you. I began doubting myself and mused, "What about my qualifications? Education? Corporate accomplishments? Do they even matter? Are people ready for an Asian? Am I out of my league? Will my corporate experience translate?" To stop the growing self-doubt, I thought, "I can do this. I am no stranger to adversity." But the chip I carried on my shoulder that has powered me through so many challenging obstacles collided with the hard truths of my inexperience in political campaigning. I had to pick up an endorsement before moving on to step two of Google's advice for running a successful campaign.

15

NOT THE SMILING ASIAN

I reached out to the outgoing councilman to seek his advice. He was very friendly and kind, told me I was a good candidate but that he had already given his three endorsements away and couldn't rescind his promises. He said he never knew I was even interested in running for office but told me to be visible at future council meetings to get familiar with what's going on in the city so I would come across as a serious candidate. The logic of his advice didn't really make sense to me. Since the council meetings were generally attended by councilmembers themselves, staff, and a few interested citizens, what were the advantages of showing up if none of them were endorsing me? By showing up, I would be demonstrating to them that I was deferential to them, and I was not. While all the potential candidates turned out at every meeting, I never bothered to attend.

A week later, I attended a high school basketball game to let some friends know that I was running for City Council.

At halftime, a key member of the La Mirada 200 approached me and began to admonish me in front of a packed crowd. I was dumbfounded and asked him why he was so angry. He said firmly, "What do you mean the current council needs new leadership?" It finally dawned on me that he was referring to one of the talking points in the walk sheet that I had started circulating to voters of the city. Having survived the battlefields of Chinatown, I was not even slightly intimidated. Instead, I stood in front of him eye to eye and told him that I was running as an original, not an extension of the current council. The drama unfolded in front of a crowded gym until one of the coaches had to separate us. During the entire fracas I never felt any animosity between us, just a lot of intensity. After the game, we ignored each other as we were leaving the gym. Before I got into my car a longtime high school booster came up to me, introduced himself, and said, "I saw what happened. You have my vote."

At another community event, while I was trying to get an endorsement from a high school baseball coach, another La Mirada 200 leader physically interjected himself right in the middle of our conversation and blocked me from making further eye contact with the coach. After the event, I confronted him and told him that if he were to be so blatantly disrespectful again, my actions would be different. His face turned ghostly white, and he told me he didn't know he was interrupting a conversation. I sternly gazed into his eyes and repeated what I said with force. I wanted him to know that this sickly boy who grew up in the streets of

Chinatown and survived the beatings from gangs would not be intimidated with these white-collar tactics. My parents suffered through their silence and took it. Not me. But the ugliness of campaigning was just getting started.

At this point, I told Cathy I needed her help in running my invisible campaign because in reality, I didn't have one. She set up a meeting with a college friend who was a veteran politician from a nearby city for his advice. In my mind, he was going to impart his wisdom and strategies, but throughout the meeting, he just kept asking and writing down names and contact information of a handful of supporters from my small rolodex. At the time, I didn't know why he insisted on the precise spelling of my contacts, but I was happy to share with him the few names that I had. I found out later that he had subsequently reached out to a few of my connections, and one of them eventually later became his donor.

Tired from all the rejections and political games, I reached out to a couple of coveted unions for their endorsements and never even got a call back from any of them. After so many unsuccessful starts, I needed to do something to gain traction. I called up six of my closest Asian friends in the city to get their support. Although they would have supported me regardless of their ethnicity, I chose them as my formal campaign team to start implementing my covert plan, which in reality, consisted of my resume.

There were eight of us at Panera, and we took over the center table. None of us had any experience running a political campaign. When I told the team what I wanted to do and handed out a flyer with my vision, qualifications, and education, they all just nodded and said they would support me. But I didn't know where to start or how to lead them in this endeavor.

In my peripheral vision, I saw a man who had been listening to us intently without saying a word. It turned out Chris was a political enthusiast who brought experience that we didn't have. Chris walked over, introduced himself, and with a confident smile, he said, "Do you need my help?" Looking for a lifeline for my campaign, I said, "Sure!" Chris proceeded to hand out a thick ream of paper filled with names and addresses. He said assuredly, "Here is what you need to do. Call people up for endorsements, ask people for donations, get lawn signs, prepare mailers, and start knocking on doors." I interrupted him and said, "I did call some people, but they all said no." He continued without acknowledging my objections, "Here is what is going to happen. You will be invited to a series of town hall debates to talk about your qualifications and why you are the best candidate to win the open seat." While we listened intensely, he emphasized, "Seven of you are vying for three open seats, but in reality, the two incumbents are going to get re-elected. So essentially, it is five of you fighting for one open seat."

I looked around and saw that the initial excitement in the room had completely wilted in silence, like a balloon deflating right before my eyes. I felt defeated before the battle even began. In my mind, I was thinking, "Is this even worth my time? Maybe I should just end my campaign now and save myself the embarrassment of coming in last."

Without missing a beat, Chris looked at my leaflet and said, "You have zero name recognition. You need to run a different strategy than anyone else." Chris explained that since La Mirada had never had an Asian candidate before, I would need to endear myself to the audience. He said solemnly, "During a debate, you should try not to over-engage, but rather, to just smile when you are asked questions that you don't have the answer to." At this moment, I felt like Hamilton when Aaron Burr counseled him to "Talk less, smile more, and don't let them know what you are about."

The math-oriented, quiet, hard-working stereotypical Asian that I was supposed to perpetuate just didn't sit well with me. Cathy was visibly upset at this point. She had her arms folded in front of her, ready to explode. Chris also strongly recommended that I should get rid of all my educational achievements since I was not running to be on a school board. My friend Jun, who usually is very mild mannered, spoke up immediately. "I am not a politician, but I disagree with you. I think Ed's passion for education is one of his strong points, and we should leave his educational accomplishments in." Without skipping a beat, Chris went on and urged that I replace the colorful tie and shirts on my handout with a solid-colored tie and muted-color shirt because politicians were not supposed to look stylish.

We were all acquiescent at this point. Sensing the depleted energy level and seeing the pained expressions and drooped shoulders, I was prepared to end my campaign at this point. I thought to myself, "I am no smiling Asian, in fact, I am an extremely extroverted person, and I love my colorful ties. Is this what I have to do to even have a chance at the one open seat? Is this even what I want? I don't want to be someone I am not if that's what I have to do. I would rather just bow out." Before I adjourned the meeting, one of my friends said, "Maybe there is a better way. I know someone who ran successful campaigns before and if you are still up to it, I can set up an appointment and we can get some guidance from him." With no other viable options, I said in a barely audible tone, "Sure." We ended the evening with an appointment with Kevin as a last attempt to resuscitate my rapidly vanishing campaign. It was a quiet drive home. I felt discouraged, stymied, and defeated.

The next day, the five of us met with Kevin for lunch at a restaurant known for their linguini and clams. The meeting was supposed to give my campaign the adrenaline jolt I desperately needed for a restart. We made inconsequential small talk during lunch, but Kevin didn't ask a lot of questions about me or my campaign. After the sumptuous lunch, with my notepad and $1 Bic pen in hand, I waited patiently for his pearls of wisdom. Finally, Kevin looked at me and said impassively, "So you are the new candidate for La Mirada City Council?" Hoping to raise his energy level to equal mine, I responded enthusiastically, "Yes, I am!" In a dispassionate monotone, Kevin explained, "Since you don't have any name recognition, you have to give people a reason to talk about you. My advice is to temporarily suspend your campaign, and then two weeks before the election, flood the city with lawn signs to shock people into talking about you."

I put my notepad and pen down, mused over what he said, and the engineer in me thought, "This strategy makes absolutely no logical sense." Without missing a beat, he continued, "Use the lowest grade paper you can find to portray humility, so it doesn't come across like you are trying to buy the election." Finally, he said, "You might have a slim chance to pull this off, but if your wife runs, she will win. She is beautiful and an educator. People will gravitate toward her naturally." I was livid but somehow able to keep my composure. Kevin's hogwash advice quickly replaced the sweetness of the briny and succulent clams. The only thing I agreed with him on during the entire two-hour ordeal was that my wife is beautiful and a passionate educator. I immediately asked for the check, reluctantly paid for lunch, and we politely said our goodbyes.

As soon as we got into the car, we looked at each other and simultaneously said, "What a waste of time that was." But being the eternal optimist that she is, Cathy said, "At least we found a great place to have linguini and clams!" The restaurant did eventually become one of our favorite go-to eateries. In the middle of our conversation, my phone rang, and it was Chris calling. He left a three-minute-long message which I promptly deleted. I didn't need any more self-proclaimed political pundits injecting more senseless rubbish into my campaign.

I was disappointed that I was not able to generate more buzz for my campaign. But I knew I had one last attempt at the Chili Holiday, a well-attended event with thousands of people coming through our city's beautiful waterpark for free chili dogs and hot cocoa. All the incumbents and hopeful candidates were there to mingle with the attendees, hoping to get endorsements and votes. Cathy and I got there around 8 p.m., two hours after the event had already started. We managed to tell a few friends that I would be running for a position on city council.

Near the end of the event, a staff member tapped me on my shoulder and told me I was summoned by Madison, one of the city's early founders. When I greeted her, she looked at me with her piercing brown eyes and asked, "Why didn't you ask for my endorsement before you decided to run?" I said, "I had no idea who you were and if I had asked, would you have endorsed me?" She said firmly, "No." Without any hesitation, I said, "Then why would I come check with you?" She said, "You have spunk, young man. I like you." She smiled warmly at me and said, "Would you be willing to come to my house for a cup of coffee next week? Write down my phone number and home address, come around 9 a.m., and I will make you some of my unrivaled coffee." I thought, what the heck, I have nothing to lose and told her, "Sure!"

On the way out, we ran into the spouse of one of the La Mirada 200 leaders, who had already rejected my request for his endorsement weeks ago. She sympathetically said, "You should just use this race as a learning experience, get your name out there, then try again next time." Essentially, she had already written me off. I began to wonder if everyone felt the same way. It was another silent car ride home. Even though the radio was on high volume, her words of denouncement kept replaying in my head like a broken record.

I would never run for city council just for name recognition so that I could do it again four years later. I ran because I felt I could bring a unique set of skills that could make an immediate impact on our great city. I run to win! But my confidence was eroding, and I was doubting my chances of winning. What the hell did I get myself into? Should I just quit the race? When we got home, Cathy simply said, "When do we start?" Her soothing voice injected some much-needed cortisone into my immune-compromised campaign.

I began to seriously evaluate the situation to determine whether I should quit or stay in the race to the end. Based on past experience and data, incumbents won reelection every time in the absence of any scandals. In essence, it was five challengers running for one open seat, so each of us had a 20 percent chance of winning. I started appraising my chances of winning against the other challengers. The frontrunner was the anointed heir apparent to the outgoing councilman. He was the envy of everyone, including myself. Another challenger had deep roots in La Mirada and proclaimed himself Mr. La Mirada, the native son. Further bolstering the profile of challengers was an attorney, former veteran and law enforcement officer. He had previously run for a council position and was a good campaigner. The final challenger was the father of an incumbent councilman, an outspoken critic of the city. His son was already a councilmember who unsettled the current makeup of the council by beating an incumbent who was embroiled in some controversy. Now his dad wanted to serve side by side with his son to dismantle the current bureaucracy.

I was the rookie, had no political connections, and basically the freshman challenger. I also had the stigma of history against me—that no Asian had ever run for a councilmember seat. But strangely, I was consumed with the image of my mom struggling up the hill with heavy bags in each hand. I thought, "My parents didn't quit on us when they were faced with overwhelming odds. This is nothing compared to what they had to go through. After all, not only am I a battle-tested kid who grew up in the rough streets of

Chinatown, but I'm also a former business executive and know how to create brands." That was it! I had to create my own brand, craft the right message that would emotionally resonate with voters, and tell the right story to the right audience. What did I have to lose? The expectation of me winning, including myself, was so low that if I lost, it was expected.

16

THE CAPELESS HEROES

The challenge in a campaign is whether we can get people to think differently about something or someone. Could I change Madison's mind with my personality, humility, and intelligence? She was stubborn, tough, and had already made up her mind.

It was a sunny Monday morning in the suburbs, and as I pulled up to Madison's driveway and got out of my car, the scent of the color green instantaneously wafted into my nostrils. Her front yard was immaculately cut with fresh mower tracks laid out in a contrasting light-dark checkerboard stripe pattern. I tipped my head back, took a big whiff, and hoped to savor the sweet fragrance of freshly cut grass before being punched in the face by symptoms of red eyes, an itchy nose, and sneezing. Somehow, the aroma of green nature automatically conjures up the feeling of hope, of a chance of a new beginning for me.

Not knowing what to expect, I gently knocked on her door and before the second tap, Madison opened the door and greeted me with a welcoming smile on her face. She said with a devious grin, "I have been waiting for you. What were you doing lingering on my lawn?" Before I could respond, she said eagerly, "Come try my coffee." She then gently held my hand and led me into her office, which was essentially a small round dining table in her kitchen. No longer sitting on a wheelchair as she did when I first met her at the Chili Holiday, she looked slender, vibrant, and fashionable with distinctive accessories.

Inside her kitchen office, I noticed that the entire table was covered by the various sections of the *Times*. As she was pouring me a cup of her signature decaffeinated brew, she turned her attention to the newspaper and told me that she reads every article of the *Times* from cover to cover each morning. After some casual chitchat, she asked me why I was running. I told her about my upbringing and motivation for running without holding back. When I was done, she surprisingly said to me, "I am changing my mind and endorsing you." Although it was only one vote, it was a start!

A week later, I unexpectedly received a $500 check in the mail from a family we didn't know, and Cathy and I tracked them down and thanked them for their generous donation in person. That was a major confidence booster. It turned out they were prominent members of the community. I found out years later that Madison had contacted them and told them to support me. Not all storms come to disrupt your life, some come to clear your path.

Madison and I became close friends through the years. She adored Cathy and was like a second mom to her. A young spirit that she was, Madison passed away in 2020. I will always remember her wit, spunk, and humor. She had secured her legacy as the queen of La Mirada and will be cherished as a guardian of a city that she loved so much.

In the official ballot statement, I decided to include education as one of my top priorities even though I had no control over the schools. Several members of the La Mirada 200 told me that they would support me if I was to run for the school board but not for city council. However, my affinity for education attracted one school board member, and even though she had never met me before, she reached out to me and gave me my first endorsement from an elected official. A week later, a former councilman and his wife invited me to their home and after some benign tittle-tattle, I received my second endorsement from an elected official. Although I could count all of my endorsements on one hand at this point, I was feeling more confident than at any time during my futile campaign.

I finally bought a voters list from a political database vendor. It took Cathy several weeks to organize the database and map out all the walking routes. Throughout the project, she jokingly reminded me several times that I had said she didn't need to be involved since I would take care of everything. After some bantering, I told her that I was so thankful for her unequivocal support, that without her, I wouldn't even know where to begin. She jokingly said, "I had done this back in my college days, but I thought that phase was over." She paused and said, "Show La Mirada who Ed Eng is." My eyes became misty, and I quickly turned away from her before any tears spilled over onto my cheeks. I was just so appreciative of her unwavering confidence in me. I silently told myself, "I will not let her down. Even in defeat, I will bring honor to my family. I will fight to the end."

I had been very active in Brandon's life both in sports and academics. In sports, I gave all the kids that I had coached, including the underdogs, a chance to play and the opportunity to be put in a competitive situation regardless of skill level or experience. Parents always thanked me for giving their kids confidence they didn't have before joining my teams. My involvement in Brandon's education for twelve years had also earned me a reputation for being an education advocate. I started the first Academic Booster Club at his high school and even invited news media to cover the event. Through my twelve years of involvement in sports and school, I had made several friends and countless number of acquaintances, and some of them eventually became lifelong friends. I didn't know it at the time, but I was already well known in my community, only not in the political arena. Little did I know that these relationships would pay me back in votes.

My campaign kickoff began with drizzles and, at times, torrential rain. I thought to myself, "Who is going to show up on a rainy day and walk for me?" The kickoff was supposed to start at 11 a.m., and at 10:45 a.m., we heard cars driving up and parking in front of our house. We rushed to the window, and there was the school board member who had endorsed me. She was followed by most of the friends I had invited. I was touched. The "mamacitas", the group of moms whose kids I coached in basketball, all showed up with their husbands to show their support. My original campaign team was also there to encourage me.

Everyone was given a few short routes around the neighborhood to promote me as their candidate. The mamacitas told me that when they were asked why they were supporting me, they didn't really know what to say except, "We believe in him." While we hit the ground game running, the spouses of the mamacitas were driving in the pouring rain to put up signs in street intersections, and one of them almost got run over twice. In the worst of times, my friends showed up. Their presence was better than any endorsements I could have received from anyone. I will forever be grateful to them.

After the initial kickoff, the hard work of convincing residents that I was worthy of leading a city was just beginning. Cathy and I began our campaign trail on weekends. I knew I could count on at least thirty votes by now—a far cry from the at least 2,000 votes required to win.

But the count had multiplied by six times from only a week ago. We walked in pairs, but Cathy was always way ahead of me because of how long I ended up talking to each potential voter. One former councilmember told me to spend no more than thirty seconds at each door, but I ended up spending an average of fifteen minutes to half an hour answering questions from just one household. It was a disaster in time management.

On a now routine weekend hitting the campaign trail, I ran into Sam, a neighbor who was looking for his lost dog. I had never met this neighbor before but gave him a flyer. He called me the next day and asked to be part of my campaign team; subsequently, Sam became the most prolific walker on my team. Sam walked practically every weekend, including going to hard-to-find addresses in condos and apartment units. He did that so I could have time to meet as many people as possible without wasting time looking for addresses. I also received a call from Argus, a young college kid who contacted me and asked if I needed help. He ended up knocking on doors almost every weekend.

Despite a grueling walk schedule of pounding the pavements every weekend, I didn't feel like we were covering much ground. The problem was that I didn't know how to discriminate between the high- and low-propensity voters based on voting history and political affiliations. It was only after the election that I found out each voter had a code assigned to them that explained how likely they were to vote.

I treated the low-propensity voters the same as I would the high and knocked on every door that historically voted. The city became this gigantic community with never-ending streets to walk, and we were only able to cover 20 percent of the voters on the list. To make up the shortfall in the ground game, I thought maybe I would do better in the air game—the planned mailers.

The Air Game

I was told by political consultants that Friday is the optimal day for mailers to arrive in voters' mailboxes because it would give people the weekend to review the candidates' qualifications, fill out their ballots, and mail them on Monday. Following this logic, I had scheduled four sets of mailers to arrive on successive Fridays. On the Friday when my first mailer was supposed to come in, I waited patiently for mailman Bob to even out my pathetic ground game. As I sorted through credit card solicitations, coupons, and my competitors' flyers, mine was nowhere to be found. In a panic, I chased down Bob and told him what had happened and asked what I could do to remedy the situation. In a sympathetic tone, he told me to go down to the Post Office Central Distribution Center to check to see what had happened to my mailers.

I frantically navigated the Friday afternoon rush hour and made it down to the centralized distribution hub just before closing time but was told that they would look into it.

In a rage, I pointed at the motto which was chiseled onto the stone wall and pleaded with them to look for my mailers. In an apathetic tone, the supervisor told me, "We are closing in five minutes. Fill out this form and someone will call you back." I left in disgust and called Cathy to tell her what had just happened. She listened and, in a calm, soothing voice, said, "We will figure something out."

A week later, unexpectedly, the supervisor called me and told me that they had found my lost mailers in the back room because my printer had tagged them incorrectly. The supervisor told me how the postcards should be tagged and said they would be mailing them out that same day. I finally received my first mailer two weeks later than the anticipated date, which meant my second set of mailers was already two weeks behind. Even though I had met with the printer about the problem, the same thing happened with the second set of mailers. Again, my second set of postcards was delayed by two weeks. The printer explained that it was election time and a whole slew of jobs all came in at once, which negatively impacted the capacity of his presses. Not satisfied with his justification, I thought about withholding the last payment, but without a Plan B, I simply walked away. Finally, two weeks before the election, the second, third, and fourth sets of mailers all came at the same time. It was like a country Western line dance, one step forward and then two steps back.

The air strategy was an utter failure. I would have been rich if they had offered insurance for every failure in this campaign. I felt defeated. I thought to myself, "I can't win this, but I will finish the race." Not knowing what to do anymore, Cathy came up with a brilliant social media strategy to make up for my defunct air game.

Cathy created a Facebook (FB) account for me and requested all her friends to add me as their friend too. In less than twenty-four hours, I had more than 200 FB friends. She started managing my social media account and uploaded photos of our friends holding up my lawn sign outside their homes. Unexpectedly, I was getting lots of "likes" on every one of the postings. She would put up a new photo every two to three days with different people holding up my signs. The social media strategy gave me a new glimmer of hope. I thought, "I am just going to ask every one of my newfound FB friends to endorse me whether or not they live in La Mirada." The tactic worked since my walk sheet and website now boasted more than sixty endorsements, even though most of them were not La Mirada residents. But slowly, voters started calling me and wanting their names on my website, and in less than three days, the list of names had increased to more than 200.

The little success I had on social media didn't give me any confidence going into the election. I was disappointed in myself but satisfied that I ran my campaign with integrity and debated with candor and fervor. I had given everything and held nothing back. I endured the wrath of La Mirada leaders and did not crumble. I continued to move forward despite the voices of naysayers. I did not let the delay of the post office mailings keep me from finishing the race.

Although the campaign was emotionally draining, I took comfort in the fact that I had come a long way from the scared, defenseless, and helpless little boy who grew up in the side streets of Chinatown. It began as a futile campaign to change a system that did not serve my parents. They were silent immigrants because of their language barrier. But the change starts with me, and regardless of the outcome, people will come to know and understand my story.

It was emotionally draining to go the distance but along the journey, true friends stood by me, and blossoming acquaintances came out of nowhere to support me. But had I done enough to come in third place and take the open seat?

17

A HISTORIC WIN

Mail-in votes were in. I sat anxiously on a roughly padded chair. The more I fidgeted in my seat, the more the material scratched the bottom of my leg. My foot shook like a broken wind-up toy, only stopping when I used physical force. I was wearing my favorite brown sweater, which, from the back, looked like a glistening, damp navy-blue sweater. It is safe to say that I was nervous. The chamber room was at capacity. With over 100 people in the room that spilled over into the lobby, I did not believe there was enough oxygen to go around. Not feeling especially sociable, I was sitting by myself with vacant seats on both sides pretending that I was saving the seats for Cathy and Brandon. I had told Cathy and Brandon earlier in the day not to come to the evening's official canvassing of the votes since I was pessimistic and doubtful of my chances of winning.

As the numbers began to appear on the screen, my heart was beating so loud it was deafening. I knew that I would have at least three votes since Cathy, Brandon, and I all voted for me. I peeled my eyes off my name and set my sights on the numbers next to the other six names. It was thunderously quiet; a hushed murmur was audible each time a number changed on the projected screen. I was mesmerized by the rows of names and numbers as they automatically updated in real-time. After the first set of numbers came in for the first of seven precincts, I was hovering in third place by a few votes. The numbers began to change rapidly and with each subsequent precinct's numbers, the gap narrowed between the incumbents and me. From the corner of my eyes, I saw Cathy and Brandon walk in, and they both took the vacant seats next to me. Cathy gently held my hand and whispered to me, "There is no way we were going to let you go through this alone." With happy tears welling up in my eyes and a raspy voice, I told her, "Thanks for coming." After all the vote-by-mail ballots were counted, I overtook one of the incumbents and was in second place. When the vote-by-precinct votes were counted, my lead grew wider with each precinct until I took the lead.

It was a historic win—the first Asian American elected official in the city, and the first time a challenger ended up in first place with the most votes, surpassing the incumbents. The voters trusted me to run their city. I couldn't pinpoint what the reasons were or the one trigger that tilted the election in my favor, but it was inconceivable that I could have accomplished this feat on my own. There is no such thing as a self-made man or woman, and I will be forever grateful to my family, friends, and the voters who believed in me even when I doubted myself. They supported me unconditionally through the entire campaign but never sought out the credit that they deserved. I am also thankful to each of my opponents for creating the most talked about election in our city's history. Some people told me it was my candor, education, and experience that made the difference, but whatever it was, I was truly humbled to win this election.

In retrospect, I understood why a few of the La Mirada 200 leaders were upset with me. They were only trying to protect this great city that they helped build. They didn't know my motivation for running and just wanted to make sure that the city was in good hands. It also became clear to me that all the advice I received from political pundits did not have any ill intentions. They wasted precious time with me when they didn't need to do so. The tactics they devised were what they thought gave me my best chances of winning. I was just angry and felt sorry for myself when I should have been thanking them for wasting their valuable time on me.

On the day of the swearing-in ceremony, it was standing room only within the light wood-paneled walls of the council chamber. The city staff had to bring in folding chairs to accommodate the overflowing crowd. As I took my seat on the dais, I didn't know what the expectations were for a newly elected official, but I was not going to change myself to fit someone else's stereotype of how a councilmember should look, act, or speak. I was not there to test some ethnic experiment or right every wrong there was in society. I am an Asian American who speaks with candor, deals with conflicts head-on, and is undeterred by fear of criticism. I don't dress in glum colors, and yes, my wife is still beautiful. What would I do if I had lost? I guess I will never know. But I do want people to know, I am not a smiling Asian.

The Passing of a Matriarch

I invited all my family members and friends who supported me in the election to my victory celebration. There were no elected officials at the party. I wanted to send a strong message that I would not be beholden to anyone, including those constituencies that determine success at the polls. I would govern with no allegiance to anyone and make decisions without fear of any political consequences. During my speech, I got pretty choked up knowing that my mom would not be there to celebrate this historic day with me.

She passed away on May 12, 2013, after suffering a massive heart attack which eventually led to kidney failure. It happened so fast. One night after dinner, she complained of shoulder pains, and knowing that she never complained about any sort of discomfort, we immediately knew it was serious and took her to the hospital. The emergency care physician reviewed her medical history, had my mom perform some rotational movements around the shoulder region, and determined that her intense twinges were just arthritis inflammation. She was sent home after a shot of painkillers and some industrial-strength Tylenol.

That night the pain worsened, and she began vomiting but downplayed her pain level while struggling to put on a smile. We didn't want to take any more chances and brought her back to the hospital, only this time, we demanded more comprehensive tests. Three hours later, the doctor informed us that my mom had suffered a massive heart attack and required immediate surgery. Later that evening, she had surgery and ended up staying in the hospital a couple of weeks for recovery. Her health deteriorated gradually after that. Eventually, her kidneys were so severely damaged that she needed full-time dialysis. Her condition became terminal and during all this time, she never complained about any pain or discomfort. She was the strongest person I knew. While her body gave up on her, her spirit to fight never wavered. To the end, she fought fiercely even when she had lost thirty pounds off her already petite frame. The last thing she said to my dad was, "The struggle was so worth it." Six powerful words that embodied their sacrifice for us and love for each other.

It was the passing of the matriarch for our clan. She was not alone before she ascended to heaven. Brandon and his cousin Kevin were holding each of her hands as she took her last breaths. With each weakened breath, her legacy was passed onto future generations. I spoke fondly of her at the funeral. My voice crumbled and composure faltered as I spoke about the love and care she had for me. I will forever be grateful for all the times she held my hands or caressed my forehead when I was sick to let me know she was there. I will miss her incessant inquiry of "Have you eaten yet?" and I will always celebrate her not only for her selfless love but for her audacious strength and courage to overcome challenges. Those are the foundational values that have carried me through tough times.

Mom's departure and absence left an aperture in my heart, but her indomitable spirit of courage and fight was a gift I would like to share with the world. The image of her walking up the hill carrying bags of zippers and pants in each hand was a reminder of the sacrifice my parents made to give me the life that they didn't have. Her small but powerful image will forever be a torch inside of me. Most of all, I want to thank her for taking care of this fragile little boy and for her sacrifice so that we could all have a piece of the Gold Mountain. I love you, Mom!

18

THE SECOND CAMPAIGN

After winning a seat on the city council in 2015, I asked myself, "What is the next thing that I want to accomplish more than anything?" I had taught part-time at a couple of universities and really enjoyed the experience, so unquestionably, it was to get a doctoral degree. But since I was at the tail end of my professional career, what would I do with it? The short answer was anything I want or nothing at all.

Throughout my school years, the fear of making mistakes and studying just to get a good grade chipped away at the curiosity within me. In the workplace, senior executives sacrificed experimentation for profits. I hated titles and labels because they unintentionally suppressed creativity. While the prevailing business sentiment is to be an expert in a subject area, I have been a multi-careerist whose eclectic professions included a wide variety of occupations and interests. For the first time in my life, I wanted to go to school without a specific purpose in mind, like getting a promotion, starting a business, or making more money. Traditional metrics cannot measure the return on growth at this stage of my life. I simply had a thirst for knowledge and wanted to embrace learning not just as a stage in my life but as part of my life.

To calm the raging fire inside of me, I finally decided to follow my heart and get a doctoral degree in leadership. Although I already had two master's degrees, I believed that there would be more intellectual freedom at the doctoral level. I wanted to discover new knowledge, deepen my curiosity, and be with like-minded people who had a passion for learning.

In the summer of 2017, I reached out to Pepperdine University to inquire about the process. The admissions officer asked for some personal background information, copies of my writing, and work experience, all of which I provided to them on the same day. By the weekend, I was in class for orientation. The entire process took four days. It was surreal. But it was a tough start because although I was fluent in differential calculus and business frameworks, I have never been good in academic writing. The program forced me to step out of my comfort zone from day one. For the first year, I relied heavily on Cathy and Brandon to get me through the course work. Brandon would teach me how to improve the style and structure of my writing, and Cathy would edit my papers. Eventually, I had developed my own style of storytelling in academic compositions.

Aside from research and writing papers, one of the most impactful learning moments occurred during an international policy trip to Belize. I had brought Cathy and Brandon along so I could say that I was intentionally integrating work-life balance. We went to Belize two days in advance to spend some family time together. Outside of the hotel, taxi drivers were waiting on every street corner hustling for business. Since we didn't know the area well and didn't have that much time, we decided to hire a taxi driver named Edgar to take us to remote tourist spots that only the locals knew about. We went cave diving with tubes, ate at local restaurants, and learned about the Belizean culture.

After one of the excursions, we went out to lunch, and after a couple of bites, Edgar asked to bag his food to go. Before we made our way back to the hotel, Edgar stopped by a local village and honked three times. In an instant, a group of local kids ran out to greet him. He hugged them and shared his leftover lunch with them. Edgar didn't have much, but he was willing to give what he had to his people. He told us that was the way of Belizean life.

What an impactful exhibition of leadership moment it was for me! That experiential moment resonated deep to the core of humanity, and no books could have taught me that. Edgar taught me that we all have a responsibility to lead change and make this world a better place regardless of how much or how little we have. His selfless act of kindness and compassion became the highlight of the entire doctoral program for me.

Three years went by pretty fast. The doctoral experience had opened the floodgate to infinite journals, like drinking knowledge from a fire hydrant. More importantly, it gave me the motivation to tell my own story. But the dissertation process was beginning to take its toll on me. It was a solitary process that tested my mental stamina. After reading thousands of peered-review journals, I was wondering if I had the endurance to finish the journey. I also had to make a decision whether I was going to run for reelection. If I chose to run again, that meant I would have to finish my dissertation and campaign simultaneously, which would be a Herculean effort. At this point in my life, I had the financial security to live comfortably ever after, and I didn't really want the mental stress that came with having to do both. Standing at a crossroads, I reminded myself that I was too complacent and risk-averse when Tribune first acquired the *Times* and that I needed to move forward with confidence and optimism even if the future may bring about abrupt changes emotionally and psychologically.

Then an emotional lift came unexpectedly. "Is that really you?" was the subject line in an email dated April 26, 2019. It was from Ms. Crowell, my high school teacher who insisted I go to college. She somehow tracked me down after more than forty years. She wrote, "I can't believe I found you. What an exciting bio. It looks like you have been really busy and super successful." We caught up through emails and promised to meet in person soon. In her last email to me, she said, "You are a born fighter. I am so proud of you!"

I arrived at a swift decision when a challenger in my district started to make disparaging remarks about me online. He was a "talking head" who was on social media all day long, and his derogatory comments were irritating, especially when it was unfounded and unprovoked. It was all the motivation I needed to run for reelection and finish my dissertation concurrently. As a martial artist, I practice the traditional concept of "Bushido" and embrace competition as long as there is honor among contenders. I respected him and didn't engage with him until he openly posted a video on the popular social platform Nextdoor that he was running "to drain the swamp." I took issue with his brazen disrespect for everything the city had accomplished in the last five years.

I had never met my challenger before and knew nothing about him other than his campaign of a dog park in the city because that generated the most discussion on Nextdoor. As soon as someone asked a benign question, he made it part of his campaign message. Soon, he was campaigning for housing affordability, a skate park, and everything else in between. In frustration, I started posting my own comments on Nextdoor, but my challenger would cross-comment on my threads every time. He was egging me on to engage on Nextdoor before the formal debate, and unfortunately, the app did not have an option to delete his comments. I wanted to wait until the formal debate to lay out our differences, but he wanted to do it on social media. His contemptuous style lit a fire in me and was just the catalyst and fuel I needed to push myself to win for a second term.

Despite the fact that I was one of the early users of this software platform, I quickly abandoned it because most of the posts at the time were dominated by people selling merchandise and posting lost dog ads. I didn't feel it was the proper forum to engage with my constituents. But today, the app has grown to become an important tool for daily opinions that make the traditional approach of townhalls obsolete. There are no ground rules, and a few vocal members dominate the platform, and any negativity about the city can stoke public sentiment like a wildfire. There is no way to mediate the free-for-all hostility on this social app. But you cannot fear it, or it will control you.

The correct action cannot stem from fear, and I have never shied away from saying something unpopular while on the dais even if it would hurt my chances of getting reelected or how I could be perceived. That was my political philosophy: govern with steadfast leadership, unflinching candor, and evidentiary data to improve our decision-making process. If you don't have values or convictions, people will define who they think you are. While sharing differing points of view might lead to frustration and clashes, I enjoyed the process of engaging in complex issues even though they might make unpopular conversations. Because of value differences and contrary ideologies, I knew early on that I was inevitably going to disappoint some people. But I will never let politics dictate who I am and what I do even when residents threaten me with withholding their future votes.

I also understood that those attributes were far from guaranteeing me a victory and that past accomplishments are often overshadowed by the problems of the present. In many ways, a campaign is not about who has the best agendas or qualifications, but rather a duel of personalities, character, and message. I was also not naive to the fact that some people would always want a new person regardless of qualifications and accomplishments. Nonetheless, I was more confident than the first time because, with the power of incumbency and name recognition, public sentiment was all in my favor.

A Landslide Victory

By now, there was no way to put out the fire that was searing inside of me. My challenger had motivated me with his condescending approach. His platform was also in stark contrast to mine. While he ran a "vending machine" to appease everyone on social media, my vision was to balance the current requirements of our residents with the twenty-first century needs of the city. I wanted the residents to take in the breadth of the city and its potential for greatness, while using enough discipline to balance the budget for the needs of every priority, not every want.

It had been five years since my first campaign, but this time around, I knew exactly what I needed to do. I built my website, enumerated all my accomplishments, designed my mailers, organized walk sheets, ordered lawn signs, invited friends to my kickoff, and assigned volunteers to walk particular areas. I would work during the day, write my dissertation on weeknights, and knock on doors on weekends. It was a peculiar campaign. While I was talking to residents about my vision and accomplishments, my opponent was posting Instagram-worthy pictures on his social media accounts of him holding up his signs on street corners.

Just like the first campaign, the printer made an error and delivered lawn signs that were the wrong size. With no time to make any changes, I reached out to the Manzos for help, and they ended up working all night to put two signs on each wooden stick; the next day they hammered the wooden posts at busy intersections. What an amazing friend! It looked funky, but it grabbed attention because of its weirdness and odd shape. Then one weekend, sixty of my lawn signs were missing, and eight of the more prominent signs on busy intersections were slashed. I contacted law enforcement, and they set up a sting, but nothing turned up.

I was exhausted after three months. Did my hard work translate to an eventual victory?

With technology advances, we can now access real-time results on our computers without going to city hall on the day of the election. Sitting in front of my monitor, I calmly waited for the results to pop up on my screen. The first results came in at approximately 9:10 a.m. I garnered 82 percent of the votes. Without waiting for further unveiling of the counts, I turned off my computer and continued working on my dissertation. The campaign was over, and I started getting congratulatory texts throughout the night. When the results were certified, I had won with over 85 percent of the votes. But there was no celebration and no high fives, I just continued working on my dissertation which was due in less than thirty days.

A month later, on April 23, 2021, I cleared the entire dissertation process, published my manuscript, and officially became Dr. Ed Eng. Subsequently, the publisher provided a report that showed my dissertation had been downloaded more than 100 times, with most of the downloads coming from outside the US. It was a fantastic feeling to know that it was being viewed by a global audience. This is how knowledge is advanced, and this is how impact is created. Tears began streaming down my cheeks as I looked at my diploma. Again, I wished Mom was here to see that her hard work and sacrifice had paid off. I took about a week off to reflect on the past year, enjoy a couple of nice dinners with family and friends, then I was back to the book I started writing sporadically in between my doctoral studies, *The Accidental Mayor.*

To celebrate our victory, Cathy and I spent the day admiring incredible postwar artwork at the MOCA museum and following a sumptuous vegetarian Thai food dinner in Hollywood, we headed home on the notoriously stop-and-go gridlocked LA Interstate 5 freeway. As we navigated Siri's advice, we wound up taking mostly local streets to get around those ribbons of yellow and red on my traffic app. I casually mentioned that the house where I grew up was only fifteen minutes away from where we were. Since we were already delayed by the stereotypical LA traffic, Cathy asked if we could take a detour to see where and how I grew up.

The diversion took us to Belmont High School, and as we walked around the school's perimeter, it looked just like an abandoned building without much life. I started rehashing stories about gangs and fights that I had told her a million times in our thirty years of marriage. After about thirty minutes of aimless loafing, I casually told her that we were only about two miles from where I grew up and she excitedly said, "Let's go see it!"

It was a familiar scene. There it was. The lifeless pink apartment building where my family was terrorized stood hostile and stoic. I truly thought the feeling of inferiority would stop when I saw the apartment building I once called home. It did not. Instead, the memories added to the growing sense of agitation. About 100 feet away, some houses and buildings were still defaced with graffiti, and a few abandoned cars with shattered windows parked on both sides of a narrow street meant for only one car passing through at a time.

With tears in her eyes, she held my hand and whispered, "I can't believe you made it out of here. You have come a long way, babe." Those words stirred up the memories of growing up poor, being bullied at school, beaten up by gangs, and struggling to assimilate while balancing American values with those of my own culture. The image of our daily lives as first-generation immigrants was overwhelmed by desperation and survival. My parents' dream was for us to avoid the struggles they had to endure. We never took a family vacation because it was pointless to spend money on luxury experiences we couldn't afford. But when you are trudging through life's obstacles just to put food on the table, their dreams of a college education and a good-paying job for all of us seemed a galaxy away. Without an escape rope in the form of a robust social network or web of business contacts that provided social capital and opportunities, we had to rely on instincts to survive the deplorable conditions of poverty and gangs.

But those early years of survival actually made me stronger to deal with adversity. I knew that if one day I was going to have children of my own, I had to leave the neighborhood where I grew up. I felt that my only escape route was a decent education. Although I still remember the physical bumps, bruises, scars, and emotional wounds, I am now thankful for those struggles because without them, I wouldn't have discovered my identity and strengthened my values. Not every event in your life will be good, and not every story will have a fairy-tale ending. While some may even feel like a disaster, I have come to realize that there are no *real* accidents, only opportunities. A casual fishing trip led me to marry the woman of my dreams. A chance encounter at a donut mixer at city hall pointed me to politics. Somehow, those varying experiences all came together at the exact opportune time when I needed them most, and in my case, to become *The Accidental Mayor*.

One month after swearing in for my second term, the onset of the Covid pandemic wreaked havoc across the world. The apocalyptic scenes from the hit series *Walking Dead* were reenacted right before our eyes. Seemingly overnight, travel was canceled, streets were empty, and offices were shut down. A reliable Wi-Fi connection became our only connection to the world and joined air, water, and food as the now indispensable big four. In a year of Zoom burnout, mask mandates, and virtual workouts, the world yearned for a return to normalcy.

After about a year and a half of confinement to outdoor gyms, takeout, and excursions to the grocery stores, Cathy and I were finally able to take a vacation to Oahu, Hawaii. I chose the window seat so I could watch the plane take off. The reflection from the twelve-millimeter-thick acrylic windowpane was a self-assured man with emerging grays sprinkled across his already follicle-challenged hair pattern. The ebb and flow of time had left deep uneven wrinkles across his forehead like asymmetrical railroad tracks. The scar had blended in perfectly with the rest of the creases and now looked more like a derailed track trying to reconnect to the main railway system. It is now an invisible scar only I can feel. Although the wrinkles were now so pronounced, the face no longer resembled the pale and sick boy from fifty years ago.

As the plane ascended to 5,000 feet, the buildings below still looked like Lego blocks of fifty years ago, but I also saw magnificent mountains in the backdrop sprayed with sunrays across them, creating the imagery of a Gold Mountain. In an instant, I thought to myself, I have finally found my Gold Mountain: the hope that my parents had envisioned immigrating to America so that we could have a chance at a better future. When my surroundings were dark and gloomy, confined to the boundaries of my skin, it was hard to see the splendor of this world. But when we realize that we have the power to see such beauty, to reach toward the sky with big dreams, we can truly embrace our own Gold Mountain.

REFLECTION

*I am no longer a scared, sickly immigrant
boy. I am not afraid to dream, fail,
or succeed.*

The catalyst for writing this book was sparked by my entrance into politics. I will be quite honest with you, I dreamed of working on Wall Street and never aspired to become a politician. While I am gregarious and outgoing (the type to make friends with people while standing in line at the grocery store), I did not ever think I could convince thousands of people to entrust their well-being to my decisions. This mindset did not come from a lack of confidence, but I truly had no desire to assume the public scrutiny, criticism, and ideological divisions that came with being a politician. I wanted to be "Edward, my neighbor" not "Edward, my mayor."

What began as a compilation of memorable lessons in the form of one- or two-sentence scribbles has evolved into a bevy of personal stories that informed the various inflection points of my life. In the hopes that one day, my son could laugh at my many mistakes and learn from them, I decided to turn these scribbles into compelling stories that would outlive me. Looking back at my life, I have come to realize, yet still do not fully understand, that there are no *real* accidents. Every event is somehow interconnected.

By reliving the emotional moments of each chapter, it was crystal clear I also wrote this book to pay tribute to my parents, who sacrificed so much to give me the life I have now. They taught me never to underestimate human adaptability and the capacity to survive. They fought for what mattered to them—their children. Their singular purpose of a better life for us gave them the motivation to overcome all insurmountable odds. They lived an impoverished life but never wallowed in self-pity amid financial hardship and dire circumstances. Even when they were beaten down, humiliated, and suffered, they never gave up. They passively navigated roadblocks the hard way and gave away their chance at a simpler yet more comfortable life in Hong Kong so that we had a real first chance at life's opportunities in America. My success resulted from their emotional strength and physical stamina to not give up, and I was not ever going to waste it.

My immigrant story is not unique, and the lessons, I would argue, are universal. We were faceless immigrants who left our home seeking better opportunities by adopting

America as our home. But it was not an easy path. The stories we plan and the way they actually play out are often two very different things. The language barrier that hamstrung my parents' upward mobility did not hamper their dreams. From watching my parents struggle, I learned that there are no magic wands that could make all the discomforts go away. Many mysteries in life defied explanations. But life also has a way of giving us a victory after every loss and vice versa. Every hill and valley follow one another, resembling a turning point in your life; whether it is a success, failure, or lesson learned will depend on your perspective and the action you take at each turn.

With this internal lens, I began to value life's wrong turns and the plethora of mistakes and not spend too much time overanalyzing and trying to make sense of events that were happening to me, good or bad. I soon realized that every small failure would prepare me to face a bigger debacle, and over time, these catastrophes became less daunting, until eventually, my most epic failures became the catalysts to my most extraordinary stories. In the same manner, every success propelled me to take on greater risks. That is the accidental mindset.

Despite many false starts, I am now Dr. Eng, which represents the highest echelon in the academic world. However, the PhD (poor, helpless, and defenseless) I acquired growing up in a one-bedroom, roach-infested apartment in Hong Kong and enduring the perilous streets of Chinatown in the lowest moments of my life formed the main constituent parts of my journey. The events that I believed were horrible mistakes, blunders, and failures ended up teaching me so much about myself and the world around me, and I became successful because of them, not in spite of them. I could have never imagined in my wildest dreams that I would end up as the mayor of a city, much less the mayor of a city in America.

I admit, plenty of tears were shed while recounting every struggle, fear, and triumph in this book. But old wounds can hurt you only if you dwell on them. Success and failure both require the right mindset and skillsets. Self-belief, self-confidence, and grit are the dimensions that everyone must develop and nurture. By sharing these serendipitous events that happened in my life, I hope you will begin to embrace the unique journey that only you can live.

So, for those who are going through tough times, especially the little "Ed Engs" out there, don't give up hope. Believe in yourself. Dream big, persevere through obstacles, and don't be afraid to defy the odds, no matter how daunting it looks. When life pushes against your comfort zone, you push back. You just keep pushing on until you finish the race. It won't be easy. The oscillating pattern of high and low moments will continuously test our values and level of grit. But don't wait until all your fears melt away before acting because your most powerful testimonies are sometimes on the other side of your fears. Embrace every failure and success because each one will come back to help you in some way when you least expect it. If this sickly immigrant boy can do it, you can too.

The Accidental Mayor is my journey to becoming the mayor of a city, but it is not the end of my story.

ABOUT THE AUTHOR

Dr. Ed Eng was the mayor of La Mirada (2017, 2022), a business professor, and a seasoned executive with 25+ years of diverse industry experience in government, media, consulting, and engineering.

Previously, Dr. Eng was the regional president of the *Los Angeles Times*. During that time, he received the Innovator of the Year Award for his ethnic partnership strategy that catapulted the *Times* to become the largest metropolitan daily newspaper in the country.

Dr. Eng holds a Doctorate in Organizational Leadership, an MBA, an MS, and a BS in Engineering. He is a dedicated practitioner of mixed martial arts and resides in La Mirada with his wife Cathy and son Brandon.

Made in the USA
Las Vegas, NV
21 November 2022